D. H. Lawrence
Interviews and Recollections

Volume 2

Also by Norman Page

Dickens: *Bleak House* (*editor*)
Dickens: *Hard Times, Great Expectations* and
Our Mutual Friend – Casebook (*editor*)
E. M. Forster's Posthumous Fiction
Hardy: *Jude the Obscure* (*editor*)
Speech in the English Novel
Tennyson: Interviews and Recollections (*editor*)
The Language of Jane Austen
Thomas Hardy
Thomas Hardy: the Writer and his Background (*editor*)
Wilkie Collins: the Critical Heritage (*editor*)

D. H. LAWRENCE

Interviews and Recollections

Volume 2

Edited by

Norman Page

Professor of English
University of Alberta

Barnes & Noble
Totowa, New Jersey

First published 1981 by
THE MACMILLAN PRESS LTD
London and Basingstoke
Companies and representatives
throughout the world

First published in the USA 1981 by
BARNES & NOBLE BOOKS
81, Adams Drive
Totowa, New Jersey 07512

MACMILLAN ISBN 0 333 27082 7

BARNES & NOBLE ISBN 0 389 20070 0

Printed in Hong Kong

Contents

Acknowledgements

The editor and publishers wish to thank the following who have kindly given permission for the use of copyright material:

George Allen & Unwin (Publishers) Ltd, for the extracts from Bertrand Russell's *Autobiography*, vol. II: *1914–1944*.
Associated Book Publishers Ltd, for the extract from *D. H. Lawrence* by Hugh Kingsmill, published by Methuen and Co. Ltd.
Cambridge University Press and the Estate of the late Helen Corke, for the extracts from her book *In Our Infancy: an Autobiography*.
Jonathan Cape Ltd, Sophie Partridge Trust and Holt, Rinehart and Winston Inc., for the extract from *Carrington: Letters and Extracts from her Diaries*, edited by David Garnett.
Frank Cass & Co. Ltd, for the extracts from *D. H. Lawrence: a Personal Record* by E. T. (Jessie Chambers).
Chatto & Windus Ltd and Harcourt, Brace, Jovanovich Inc., for the extracts from *The Golden Echo*, © 1953, and *The Flowers of the Forest*, © 1955, by David Garnett.
Chatto & Windus Ltd and Harper & Row, Publishers, Inc., for the extracts from *The Letters of Aldous Huxley*, edited by Grover Smith; copyright © 1969 by Laura Huxley and Grover Smith.
Chatto & Windus Ltd and Viking Penguin Inc., for the extracts from the introduction to *The Letters of D. H. Lawrence*, edited by Aldous Huxley; © 1932 by the Estate of D. H. Lawrence; © renewed 1960 by Angelo Ravagli and C. Montague Weekley.
A. W. Coates, on behalf of Dr J. D. Chambers, Mrs Olive Hopkin, and the University of Wisconsin Press, for the extracts from *D. H. Lawrence: a Composite Biography*, vol. 1, edited by Edward Nehls.
Rosica Colin Ltd, on behalf of the Estate of Richard Aldington, for the extract from *Life for Life's Sake*.
Curtis Brown Ltd, New York, for the extract from *Memoirs of a Polyglot* by William Gerhardi.
Faber & Faber Ltd and Alfred A. Knopf Inc., for the extracts from *Ottoline: the Early Memoirs of Lady Ottoline Morrell* and *Ottoline at Garsington: Memoirs of Lady Ottoline Morrell, 1915–1918*, both edited by R. Gathorne-Hardy.
Granada Publishing Ltd, for the extracts from *Two Memoirs* by J. M. Keynes, published by Rupert Hart-Davis Ltd in 1949.

Harper & Row, Publishers, Inc., for the extracts from *Journey with Genius* by Witter Bynner (The John Day Co. Inc.); © 1951 by Witter Bynner.

William Heinemann Ltd and Farrar, Straus & Giroux Inc., for the extract from *The Priest of Love* by Harry T. Moore; © 1954, 1962, 1974 by Harry T. Moore.

David Higham Associates Ltd, on behalf of Ford Madox Ford, and Liveright Publishing Corp., for the extracts from *Return to Yesterday*; © 1932 by Ford Madox Ford; © renewed 1959 by Janice Ford Biala.

David Higham Associates Ltd, on behalf of Malcolm Muggeridge, for 'An Interview with Helen Corke' from *The Listener, 25* July 1968.

London Magazine, for 'Lawrence in Bandol' by Brewster Ghiselin, from *London Magazine*, no. 5, December 1958; and the extracts from 'Conversations with Lawrence' by Brigit Patmore, from *London Magazine*, no. 4, June 1957.

Macdonald and Jane's Publishers Ltd, for the extract from *Life Interests* by Douglas Goldring.

Maxwell Aley Associates, on behalf of the Estate of Ford Madox Ford, for the extracts from *Portraits from Life: Memories and Criticisms.*

Henry S. Monroe and the Modern Poetry Association, for the extract from *Poetry*, no. 34, May 1930.

A. D. Peters & Co. Ltd, on behalf of Rebecca West, for the extract from *Ending in Earnest: a Literary Log.*

Laurence Pollinger Ltd and the Estate of the late Mrs Frieda Lawrence Ravagli, for the extracts from *Not I, but the Wind* by Frieda Lawrence.

Anne Powys-Lybbe, on behalf of John Manchester, for the extracts from *Lawrence and Brett: a Friendship.*

The Society of Authors as the literary representative of the Estate of John Middleton Murry, for the extracts from *Reminiscences of D. H. Lawrence* and *Son of Woman.*

Times Newspapers Ltd, for the extract by John Middleton Murry from *The Times Literary Supplement,* 13 May 1930.

Viking Penguin Inc., for the extract from *Writers at Work: the 'Paris Review' Interviews,* second series (1963), edited by G. Plimpton.

A. P. Watt Ltd, on behalf of the Estate of Cecil Gray for the extracts from *Peter Warlock: a Memoir of Philip Heseltine.*

Weidenfeld & Nicolson Ltd, for the extracts from *D. H. Lawrence: Novelist, Poet, Prophet,* edited by Stephen Spender.

Florence*

REBECCA WEST

[Lawrence] was staying in a poorish hotel overlooking what seems to me,
since I am one of those who are so enamoured of Rome that they will not
submit themselves to the magic of Florence, to be a trench of drab and
turbid water wholly undeserving of the romantic prestige we have given
the Arno. Make no mistake, it was the hotel that overlooked the Arno, not
Lawrence. His room was one of the cheaper ones at the back. His sense of
guilt which scourged him perpetually, which was the motive-power of his
genius, since it made him inquire what sin it was which he and all mankind
have on their conscience, forbade him either enjoying comfort or having
the money to pay for it, lest he should weaken. So it was a small, mean
room in which he sat tapping away at a typewriter. Norman Douglas[1]
burst out in a great laugh as we went in and asked if he were already
writing an article about the present state of Florence; and Lawrence
answered seriously that he was. This was faintly embarrassing, because on
the doorstep Douglas had described how on arriving in a town Lawrence
used to go straight from the railway station to his hotel and immediately sit
down and hammer out articles about the place, vehemently and
exhaustively describing the temperament of the people. This seemed
obviously a silly thing to do, and here he was doing it. Douglas's laughter
rang out louder than ever, and malicious as a satyr's.

But we forgot all that when Lawrence set his work aside and laid himself
out to be a good host to us. He was one of the most polite people I have ever
met, in both naïve and subtle ways. The other two knew him well, but I
had never seen him before. He made friends as a child might do, by shyly
handing me funny little boxes he had brought from some strange place he
had recently visited; and he made friends too as if he were a wise old
philosopher at the end of his days, by taking notice of one's personality,
showing that he recognised its quality and giving it his blessing. Also there
was a promise that a shy wild thing might well give and exact from its
fellows, that he would live if one would let him live. Presently he settled
down to give, in a curious hollow voice, like the soft hoot of an owl, an
account of the journey he had made, up from Sicily to Capri, from Capri to

* From *Ending in Earnest: A Literary Log* (New York: Doubleday, Doran, 1931)
pp. 266–76.

Rome, from Rome to Florence. There seemed no reason why he should have made these journeys, which were all as uncomfortable as cheap travelling is in Italy, nor did there seem any reason why he was presently going to Baden-Baden. Yet, if every word he said disclosed less and less reason for this journeying, it also disclosed a very definite purpose. These were the journeys that the mystics of a certain type have always found necessary. The Russian saint goes to the head of his family and says goodbye and takes his stick and walks out with no objective but the truth. The Indian fakir draws lines with his bare feet across the dust of his peninsula which describe a diagram, meaningless to the uninitiated, but significant of holiness. Lawrence travelled, it seemed, to get a certain Apocalyptic vision of mankind that he registered again and again and again, always rising to a pitch of ecstatic agony. Norman Douglas, Reggie Turner,[2] and I, none of whom would have moved from one place to another except in the greatest comfort procurable and with a definite purpose, or have endured a disagreeable experience twice if we could possibly help it, sat in a row on the bed and nodded. We knew that what he was doing was right. We nodded and were entranced.

The next day Norman Douglas and I went a walk with Lawrence far out into the country, past the Certosa. It was a joy for me to leave the city, for I cannot abide trams and Florence is congested with them. Impossible to pass through the streets without feeling that one is being dogged by a moaning tram one had betrayed in one's reckless youth; and it had been raining so hard that there had for long been no opportunity to walk in the country. Now there had been a day's sunshine, and the whole world was new. Irises thrust out of the wet earth like weapons suddenly brought into action. The cypresses, instead of being lank funereal plumes commemorating a foundered landscape, were exclamation marks drawn in Chinese ink, crying out at the beauty of the reborn countryside. About the grassy borders of the road there was much fine enamel work in little flowers and weeds as one has seen it on the swards of Botticelli. Of the renascent quality of the day Lawrence became an embodiment. He was made in the angelic colours. His skin, though he had lived so much in the Southern countries, was very white, his eyes were light, his hair and beard were a pale luminous red. His body was very thin, and because of the flimsiness of his build it seemed as if a groove ran down the centre of his chest and his spine, so that his shoulder blades stood out in a pair of almost wing-like projections. He moved quickly and joyously. One could imagine him as a forerunner, speeding faster than spring can go from bud to bud on the bushes, to tell the world of the season that was coming to save it from winter. Beside him Norman Douglas lumbered along stockily. Because he knew what emperor had built this road and set that city on a hill, and how the Etruscans had been like-minded in their buildings before him, he made one feel that there have been so many springs that in effect there is no spring, but that that is of no great moment. Bending over a filemot-coloured flower that he had not seen since he found it on Mount Olympus, his face grew nearly as tender as a mother bending over her child. When a child tumbled at his feet from the terrace of an olive orchard, his face became neither more nor less tender than before. They moved in unison of pace along the road, these two, and chatted. They were on good terms then, Ormuzd and Ahriman.[3]

We stopped for lunch at a place that was called the Bridge of Something: an inn that looked across a green meadow to a whitish river. We ate at a table on which a trellis of wisteria painted a shadow far more substantial than the blue mist that was its substance. The two men talked for long of a poor waif,[4] a bastard sprig of royalty, that had recently killed himself after a life divided between conflicting passions for monastic life, unlawful pleasures, and financial fraud. He had sought refuge at the monastery of Monte Cassino, that nursery of European culture, where St Thomas Aquinas himself was educated; but soon was obliged to flee down one side of the sugar loaf mountain while the carabinieri climbed up the other with a warrant for his arrest on charges connected with the Italian law of credit. Then he had gone to Malta, and played more fantasies on the theme of debt, till his invention was exhausted. This was the man whose recollections of service in the French Foreign Legion were published with a preface by Lawrence which provoked Norman Douglas to a savage retort that stands high among the dog fights of literary men. But then they were joined in amity while they talked of him with that grave and brotherly pitifulness that men who have found it difficult to accommodate themselves to their fellow men feel for those who have found it impossible. They broke off, I remember, to look at some lads who made their way across the meadow and began to strip by the river bank. 'The water will be icy,' said Douglas, 'it won't be warm till the snow goes off the mountains.' He began to chuckle at the thought of the shock that was coming to the boys who had been tempted by the first hot day. Lawrence let his breath hiss out through his teeth at the thought of their agony; but he seemed to find pleasure in it, as he would in any intense feeling.

Presently we rose, and went on our way. Norman Douglas took the landlord's hand and wrung it heartily, saying a fervid good-bye. Lawrence exclaimed, 'Douglas, how can you shake hands with these people!' He meant by this that the antipathy between the Northern and the Southern peoples was so great that there could be no sincere attempt at friendship with them. Douglas answered with a grin, 'Oh, it takes something off the bill next time.' He did not mean that. It was simply the first way that came to hand of saying that he would not get excited about these fine points, that in his universe every phenomenon was of equal value. We walked away. After a minute or two I looked back through the olive trees and saw the landlord standing where we had left him, sending after us a hard black Italian stare. 'Do you know, Douglas,' said Lawrence suddenly, though he had not looked back, 'I can't help thinking that the man understood English.' 'Oh no,' I said falsely, 'I'm sure he didn't.' But Douglas, laughing more deeply than ever, said, 'I got that too.' We all walked along without speaking, ill at ease, though Douglas kept his eyes crinkled as if he were still laughing. Ormuzd and Ahriman alike did not want unnecessary explosions of the forces they well knew to be latent in their universe.

Later Lawrence began to talk of the Sicilian peasants and how full of hatred and malice he had found them. There was a great tale about some old crones who had come up at twilight to his house in Taormina with some jars of honey they had wanted him to buy, and had crouched down on his terrace while he tested their goods with malignity in their eyes, in their squatting bodies. They had meant to cheat him, for it was last year's honey and ill preserved. He detected the fraud in an instant, with his sturdy wisdom about household matters, and bade them be gone. Silently they rose and filed out through his olive trees with their jars on their shoulders, with increased malignity in their eyes and in their prowling bodies, because they had not been able to cheat him. 'Such hatred!' he cried in effect. 'Such black loathing.' Again I felt embarrassed, as I did when we discovered him pounding out articles on the momentary state of Florence with nothing more to go on than a glimpse of it. Surely he was now being almost too flatly silly, even a little mad? Of course peasants try to cheat one over honey or anything else, in Italy or anywhere else, and very natural it is, considering how meagrely the earth gives up its fruits. But as for hatred and black loathing, surely this is persecution mania? I was a little unhappy about it, which was a pity, for that made an unsatisfactory ending to what was to be my last meeting with Lawrence, though mercifully not my last contact with him. For a few months ago I received a letter from him thanking me for some little tribute I had paid him during the trouble about his pictures in London. This letter showed the utmost humility in him to take notice of such a small courtesy; and it showed more than that. With marvellous sensitiveness he had deduced from a phrase or two in my article that I was troubled by a certain problem, and he said words that in their affectionate encouragement and exquisite appositeness could not have been bettered if we had spent the ten years that had intervened since our meeting in the closest friendship.

The point about Lawrence's work that I have been unable to explain save by resorting to my personal acquaintance with him is this: that it was founded on the same basis as those of his mental movements which then seemed to me ridiculous, and which, now that I have had more experience, I see as proceeding in a straight line to the distant goal of wisdom. He was tapping out an article on the state of Florence at that moment without knowing enough about it to make his views of real value. Is that the way I looked at it? Then I was naïve. I know now that he was writing about the state of his own soul at that moment, which, since our self-consciousness is incomplete, and since in consequence our vocabulary also is incomplete, he could only render in symbolic terms; and the city of Florence was as good a symbol as any other. If he was foolish in taking the material universe and making allegations about it that were true only of the universe within his own soul, then Rimbaud was a great fool also. Or to go further back, so too was Dante, who made a new Heaven and Hell and Purgatory as a symbol for the geography within his own breast, and so too was St Augustine, when in *The City of God* he writes an attack on the pagan world, which is unjust so long as it is regarded as an account of events on the material plane, but which is beyond price as an account of the conflict in his soul between that which tended to death and that which tended to life. Lawrence was in fact no different from any other great artist who has felt the urgency to describe the unseen so keenly that he has rifled the seen of its vocabulary and diverted it to that purpose; and it took courage to do that in a land swamped with naturalism as England was when Lawrence began to write.

When he cried out at Douglas for shaking hands with the innkeeper because the North and South were enemies, and when he saw the old crones who had come to cheat him out of an odd lira or two over the honey as maenads too venomous even to be flamboyant, I thought he was seeing lurid colours that were in his eyes and not in the universe he looked on. Now I think he was doing justice to the seriousness of life, and had been rewarded with a deeper insight into its nature than most of us have.

NOTES

Rebecca West is the pseudonym of Cicily Isabel Andrews, née Fairfield (born 1892), novelist and critic. She met Lawrence in 1921. Her recollections of him originally appeared in the *New Adelphi*, III (June–Aug 1930), and were republished as a small book, *D. H. Lawrence* (London: Martin Secker, 1930).

1. English novelist (1868–1952) resident in Italy, now best remembered for his *South Wind* (1917). The character of James Argyle in *Aaron's Rod* is based on Douglas. See also n. 4 below.

2. Prolific and now forgotten English novelist resident in Florence; a friend of Norman Douglas. Moore (p. 258) suggests that the character of Algy Constable in *Aaron's Rod* may be based on him.

3. Respectively the spirit of goodness and light and the spirit of evil and darkness in the Zoroastrian religion.

4. Maurice Magnus, an American journalist who had spent some time in the Foreign Legion. He was introduced to Lawrence by Norman Douglas in November 1919 and soon afterwards followed Lawrence to Sicily. He committed suicide in 1920. Lawrence wrote a long introduction to Magnus's *Memoirs of the Foreign Legion*, published in 1924; his essay (repr. in *Phoenix II*) precipitated a quarrel with Douglas, who attacked Lawrence in his pamphlet *D. H. Lawrence and Maurice Magnus: A Plea for Better Manners* (1924). When the pamphlet was reprinted in Douglas's collection of essays *Experiments* in 1925, Lawrence retorted in a letter to the *New Statesman* (20 Feb 1926; repr. in *Phoenix*). See also p. 246 of the present collection.

In Capri*

EARL H. BREWSTER

Lawrence had been described to me as an 'agonised soul'. I had thought of him as haggard, brooding, and sensual. Our first meeting was in Capri. How different he was from what I had imagined! How different from his own drawings of himself! These he made appear physically stronger. Instead I saw a tall delicate man. His face was pale; his hands long, narrow, capable; his eyes clear-seeing and blue; his brown hair and red beard glowing like flames from the intensity of his life; his voice was flexible, generally of medium pitch, with often a curious, plaintive note, sometimes in excitement rising high in key. He always appeared to be carelessly dressed, but it was only that apparent carelessness which arises from a fastidious nature.

That morning of which I am writing he wore a short jacket of pale homespun. He brought with him some quality of the outdoor world, from the shrubs and flowers. The sweetness of sun-dried leaves and grass seemed never to leave him. My first impression was that he looked like a man who lived devoted to the study of such life—a botanist. Immediately I felt that he was sensitive beyond others, that he knew intuitively the life of those about him, and wished to establish with them a sincere relationship. There was no condescension in his manner, his conviviality was quiet and dignified, his attitude seemed to arise from the respect which he had for the vital being one might be. Never was there the slightest sign in him of the self-conscious author.

On that first meeting we went with others to the Piccola Marina to bathe. It was a typical Mayday in southern Italy, with sun, sirocco and haze. We lay on the rocks, but Lawrence did not bathe, declaring that he did not enjoy it. He was to be in Capri only a few days.

The following morning he joined me for a walk from our house, Torre dei Quattro Venti, to the Molino, beyond Anacapri, a distance of two or three miles. It was the first occasion we were alone together. He must have known of my pre-occupation with Buddhist philosophy and its solution of the problem of suffering, for immediately upon our departure from the house he turned to me, and said:

---

* From Earl and Achsah Brewster, *D. H. Lawrence: Reminiscences and Correspondence* (London: Martin Secker, 1934) pp. 17–19.

'You don't look the intellectual type: you were not meant to be governed by the centre between your eyebrows. We should *not* pass beyond suffering: but you can find the power to endure, and equilibrium and a kind of bliss, if you will turn to the deepest life within yourself. Can't you rest in the actuality of your own being? Look deep into the centre—to your solar plexus.'

Vaguely I knew of the Hindu theory of the 'chakras', but years passed before I felt the significance of what he said to me then. Nevertheless he inspired me to tell him my intimate experiences.

He spoke of his desire for an environment where his contact with people would be more vital.

That evening before our roaring fire he was full of wit and humorous anecdotes. He was against idealism, also against what he called the attempt to overcome the tiger, whose being in us is real, he maintained, and not to be suppressed or sublimated.

NOTE

Earl H. Brewster (1878–1957) was an American painter who spent much of his life in Europe and the Far East. He and his wife Achsah met Lawrence in 1921 and remained friends with him for the rest of his life. In 1922 the Brewsters invited Lawrence and Frieda to follow them to Ceylon (see the next extract). They are depicted satirically in Lawrence's short story 'Things'.

In Ceylon*

ACHSAH BREWSTER

After our arrival in Ceylon, with much searching we had found a home of our own, 'Ardnaree'. It stood on a hill amidst great groves and jungles, high over the Lake of Kandy. Here Lawrence and Frieda joined us. Pepper-vines and crimson cocoa-pods festooned the drives, jak and bread-fruit trees spread out their green, slender areca palms shot into the air. It was a beautiful spot, with magnificent views from every side of our hill, and the broad verandahs gave each of us a quiet corner of our own. I remember their arrival and Frieda's exclaiming that it was the loveliest spot in the world and Lawrence's saying, 'I shall never leave it.' That was the first day.

* From *D. H. Lawrence: Reminiscences and Correspondence*, pp. 249–61.

They arrived carrying in their hands the side of a Sicilian cart, painted with scenes from the Palladins. They had admired these painted carts, and a Sicilian friend had taken the opportune moment to give them the broadside of one as a steamer present. The Saracens looked quite at home on our walls.

One of the first things Lawrence did was to walk around the lake, when he pulled out his watch, which had refused to go, and threw it into the middle of the lake. On his return to the house we were sitting on the north verandah for tiffin, laughing over the episode, when he touched my husband's watch-chain, admiring the design of the curious liks of silver-gold, which had been picked up in Kandy. He measured it with his eye and announced that the chain was too long—twice as much as needed, and added: 'Let me have the other half.' With delicate dexterity he pried open the links. A second fob was found and attached, making the two chains complete. Each of the two put the other half of the same chain into his own pocket.

Generally we sat on the north verandah in the morning. There was early breakfast; then tiffin; then the child went to a little school and Earl studied Pali in a monastery across the lake. Frieda, stretched out on a rattan couch, sewed and embroidered with bright silks. Lawrence sat curled up with a schoolboy's copy-book in his hand, writing away. He was translating Giovanni Verga's short stories from the Sicilian.[1] Across the pages of the copy-book his hand moved rhythmically, steadily, unhesitatingly, leaving a trail of exquisite, small writing as legible as print. No blots, no scratchings marred its beauty. When the book was finished, he wrapped and tied it up, sending it off to the publisher. All of this went on in the family circle. Frieda would come for consultation as to whether the rabbit's legs should be embroidered in yellow or white. The pen would be lifted a moment then go on across the page. Sometimes Lawrence would stop and consult us about the meaning of a word; considering seriously whatever comments were offered. He listened gravely and intently to everyone.

Each night after the child had been safely tucked into bed, after Frieda, and I had read a chapter of *Swiss Family Robinson* to her, we shivered as we walked the length of the verandah to the drawing-room. Perhaps a boa-constrictor, like the one that swallowed the donkey, would roll up his coils and bounce down upon us. We shut the door very tight and Lawrence held the lamp down to the crack to see if it were large enough for a cobra to squeeze through. He was convinced that the cobra would manage to get in. Then he would read what he had written through the day.

In the ceiling of each room was a skylight and at night not only could we hear mortal conflicts over our heads, but could see the wild-cats through the glass on the roof—five or six of them in combat. In the morning often there would be a trail of blood where a wounded snake had dragged his length. Sometimes we would hear a shot, and the watchman would announce the following day that he had killed a Russel's Viper. There was always a consciousness of teeming life, by day or night. The little mongoose and striped chipmunks ran up and down the trees; birds alighted where we sat, counting us one of themselves; crows came flapping greedily to snatch any chance morsel or glittering trinket; the trotting-bull came up on the verandah when he was thirsty. Lawrence and the child gave it water in the wash-bowl, holding it while the bull drank. The birds made a loud metallic clangour. One bird repeated an insistent crescendo eight times until the last cry was deafening. Lawrence dubbed him the 'bell of hell' and forthwith began to sing the verses of that Salvation Army hymn:

> The bells of hell go ting-a ling-a ling
> For you, but not for me.

This was done with a very personal emphasis and an air of self-righteousness. He often sang.

At six o'clock the sun gave a plunge into the lake below, with a crimson gleam that immediately sank into night. The blue hills vanished into black silhouettes and the tall areca palms swayed in the wind; the stars came out over the lake which shone below us. 'Tom-tom, tom-tom-tom; tom-tom, tom-tom-tom,' boomed up from the Temple of the Tooth through the night. We often sat on the steps leading down from the front verandah which faced the west. After its glory had faded Lawrence and Frieda would sing in the dark. For the first time there I heard them sing:

> Joseph was an old man, and an old man was he,
> And Joseph married Mary, the queen of Galilee.

Lawrence enjoyed especially the last verse where Mary retorts to Joseph: 'And *so* you see, Joseph, there *are* cherries for me!'

One morning he went to put on his topee (cork-hat), which he had taken off his head the night before, and found a family of rats had made it their home. The teeming life of the place horrified him.

When a dead leaf from the cocoanut palm fell with a crash like a bomb we all jumped in fear. There was an undercurrent of nervous dread lest something awful might happen. On moonlight nights, James the cook, the *appu*, Banda the water boy, and *ayah* assembled on the front verandah after we had gone to bed. They made *puja* to a Buddha painting, then sat cross-legged chanting. Their voices rose and fell in a strange rhythm. Lawrence would say, 'Who knows whether they are praying; they may be planning to kill us in cold blood!'

Every day on the table stood a row of six sweets—camel's milk, preserved melon, jaggery-palm sugar, cocoanut sweets invariably, and two other possibilities. The cook dished up wonderful concoctions, rich plum puddings, curries. 'How wonderful,' said Frieda. So did we all at first, then we began to shake our heads when *appu* passed them solemnly. Lawrence asked in a melancholy voice if it were necessary to have sweets of camel's milk always on the table. Then Frieda brought forth a bottle labelled 'liver-mixture' and poured out a tablespoonful for each in turn. By the next day Lawrence was heard wishing he could have a bread pudding instead of cocoanut cream with meringue on the top—those dreadful bread puddings he relished. Even with the 'liver-mixtures' the climate told on us all, especially on Lawrence, who could scarcely drag about. The season was unusually hot, yet we none of us wished to leave for the higher hills.

Immediately upon his arrival Lawrence had announced that he should tell us all our faults. His horror of repression made him believe that between friends all annoyances should be spoken forth, both to relieve oneself and to clear the situation between them. He tried to put into words what others leave tacit, even in the most trivial matter.

Hastily deciding to go to the village I asked if I were in proper order, to which he answered: 'If I were Frieda I should say you look perfectly *beautiful*! but being myself I shall say, you look *decent*.'

A workman was arranging a screen on the verandah where we were seated. He was alert; with sure, graceful movement and fine head; his dark eyes flashing; his features regular; the beard clipped in an elegant line. Lawrence pensively watched him, announcing that he resembled his father—the same clean-cut and exuberant spirit, a true pagan. He added that he had not done justice to his father in *Sons and Lovers* and felt like rewriting it. When children they had accepted the dictum of their mother that their father was a drunkard, therefore was contemptible, but that as Lawrence had grown older he had come to see him in a different light; to see his unquenchable fire and relish for living. Now he blamed his mother for her self-righteousness, her invulnerable Christian virtue within which she was entrenched. She had brought down terrible scenes of vituperation upon their heads from which she might have protected them. She would gather the children in a row and they would sit quaking, waiting for their father to return while she would picture his shortcomings blacker and blacker to their childish horror. At last the father would come in softly, taking off his shoes, hoping to escape unnoticed to bed, but that was never allowed him. She would burst out upon him, reviling him for a drunken sot, a good-for-nothing father. She would turn to the whimpering children and ask them if they were not disgusted with such a father. He would look at the row of frightened children, and say: 'Never mind, my duckies, you needna be afraid of me. I'll do ye na harm.'

Lawrence could not forgive his mother for having dragged them into those unnecessary scenes. Shaking his head sadly at the memory of that beloved mother, he would add that the righteous woman martyred in her righteousness is a terrible thing and that all self-righteous women ought to be martyred. He sat watching the workman intently; then he reiterated that there was a bit of a gleam about his father, and he wished he had done him more justice.

When a copy of *The Rainbow* appeared on the verandah he snatched it away, saying that the very sight of it was repugnant to him, it had caused him so much suffering. The public had misunderstood him always, even at college; when in his writing a paper he had used the word 'stallion', his English professor had taken him aside and said: 'My boy, that is a word we do not use.' After this reminiscence he hung his head as if in shame for the public who could not face life.

His humanity was outraged at driving in rickshaws. When, frail as he was, he needed to be carried uphill through the heat, he simply could not allow a rickshaw boy to pull him, but got out and walked.

Full of enthusiasm he would come home from the bazaars with bits of bright cotton, plaids, stripes, shot patterns of changeable colours, sandals and beads. We all would fashion them into garments. I can remember standing for hours while Frieda draped a handwoven, gold-bordered Madura saree, Earl insisting it should fall in the lines of a Tanagra figure, and Lawrence finally ripping the whole thing off to demonstrate just how many pleats there should be in the skirt, and where the folds should fall from the shoulders.

Like everyone else in Ceylon he became fascinated by precious stones. The merchants would show us their treasures and tell tales about jewels. Lawrence bought clear, bright, blue sapphires and moonstones.

In honour of the Prince of Wales'[2] visit a great *pera-hera* or religious procession of elephants was arranged. All the available elephants were collected, a hundred or more—tall dark ones with legs like palm-trees and backs like boulders; silver-grey ones speckled over their faces as if they were freckled. Richly caparisoned were they, with velvets and fringes, tassels and tinkling bells. In front of them ran attendants continually spreading out white cloth that the sacred elephants need never tread the earth. Devil dancers, some of them on stilts, performed amazing antics. Drummers and tom-tom players and pipers made strange, pulsating music. We remained until the last sky-rocket sank away into the lake. The pale prince sat in the tower of the Temple of the Tooth reviewing the procession, every elephant salaaming before him: which scene Lawrence describes in his poem '*Elephant*'.[3]

Lawrence would sit for hours pondering the new heaven of these eastern skies. He had a vivid star-consciousness, and would lament that people narrowed their view, hardly noticing the stars, not realising that they were star-doomed.

One day I asserted a belief in the communion of saints. To my surprise Lawrence rejoined that he felt a bond of deep communion with all the great and good ones of all time. Very quietly he added that angels were waiting to help man. An agonised look transformed his face as he added that often he had implored their help, but even the angels had failed him during the war.

A plump young Singhalese would come and relate tales about snakes, especially the 'honourable cobra'. Lawrence, his bright eyes watching intently to catch whatever his slightly deficient hearing might lose, listened spell-bound to records of snake suicide, their tender concern for the blind, remedies for snake-bites according to the hour of the day and the exact location of the bite and the gesture of the victim, pet cobras in school gardens milk-fed by the children. A tactful word of assent or leading question from Lawrence kept the yarn spinning. Our narrator admired Frieda, who looked to him like pictures of Buddhist saints.

She had lost a brooch given her by Lawrence. It was a hot day, which oppressed Lawrence beyond endurance, so this occurrence caused him to utter a long diatribe against the sin of carelessness; hardly had his burning words been uttered than in a low voice he recanted them all, saying gently that big things alone count and prudence spends itself in pettiness.

During the rainy season the rains came at exactly ten in the morning and four in the afternoon, timed to a minute. We knew how to calculate, except for the first one. We had started out for a walk and were well on our way, when the rain fell, not in gentle drops, but in deluges; one second had drenched us to the bone as though we had been dropped into the sea. Our hair hung like dripping seaweed, our garments clung to us so that we could barely totter, rain poured in cataracts from our cork-hats. We splashed breathlessly to the verandahs. Lawrence stood gaunt and white in the swirl of water. Although it was a tepid bath, and we were glowing with warmth after our climb uphill, still this drenching may have done us no good. As the rainy season continued we felt as mildewed as our garments in the recesses of the rooms where there was waged a continual battle against mould. Lawrence sat disconsolately, his voice reduced to a minor key, reiterating that he felt his 'heart's blood oozing away, but literally ebbing out drop by drop'. When I added that I had no cosmic consciousness or universal love left, it seemed to raise his spirits! He became quite gay and carefree at the mere thought of having lost such a load.

Lawrence was deeply conscious of our daughter, Harwood, and took an interest in her concerns, which extended even to a doll whose smashed face had been replaced by a home-made affair of a painted silk stocking. This poor substitute was dubbed by Lawrence 'Swabina' (dishcloth). This was resented:

'She's little Lucile.'
'No, that's Swabina.'
'She's Lucile.'
'Swabina!'

This anomalous doll drove about in an even more anomalous carriage created by a local carpenter. Lawrence enjoyed the sight of Swabina seated in this white hearse of a chariot that Harwood rumbled around the verandahs, and when it came time to pack he stood staunchly by her demand that she take the perambulator back to Europe with her. For this end he worked hours in the wilting heat, removing the solid wheels and

massive handles, packing them around the body of the cart which he filled
with her books. A neat arrangement but immovable!—to be inherited by
ayah's baby!

Before leaving Ceylon, as we had now decided to do shortly, we took
many excursions, motoring through the green sea of jungle. A particularly
happy trip which Lawrence enjoyed with gusto was the one up to the
heights of Nuwara Eliya. We startled a herd of deer crossing our road; the
way led first through palms and tropical plants under a hot sun, then tea
plantations. When we reached Nuwara Eliya, with its stunted pines, the
hoar frost lay thick on the ground. The bazaars of the village enticed us
within. Lawrence with one glance discovered the treasure there among the
usual tawdry array, and bore off with satisfaction some fine red lacquer
candlesticks from Cashmere painted with flowers. He turned them about,
inspecting each petal, saying that they were doubly interesting to him
because at one time he had saved all the tin boxes and glass bottles that
came his way and had decorated them with lacquer-painted flowers.

Another day, breathlessly hot, we set forth to find an isolated tribe of
people, said to be descended from kings but now outcasts, who lived in the
remote jungles. They wove reed mats with red and black designs of ducks,
elephants and other creatures. Following Lawrence's lead in single file
along a path barely visible in the rank growth, suddenly we came upon the
stinking skins of animals pegged out on the ground to dry in the sweltering
sunshine, the skins still bloody and swarming with flies. Lawrence turned
hurriedly from the sickening sight. His sensibilities were outraged.

Lawrence visited with us old rock temples where the champak flowers
were fragrant on the trees nearby. Earl and I would enter with our hands
full of the pale gold and rosy blossoms to make offerings, removing shoes
and hats to pay homage to the silent Buddha figures in the caves: coming
out, there would be Lawrence standing in his shoes, hat tight on his head,
declaring that there was no use, he did not belong there and could not join
in.

Lawrence watched the monkeys swinging from the trees, and had a
wholesome respect for the size and disposition of the elephants hauling
timber on the road.

As the days passed the heat grew worse. Our rattan beds sagged in the
middle like hammocks. We all were miserable and Lawrence could
scarcely drag about. He had been awarded a prize of one hundred pounds
for the best English novel of the season, *The Lost Girl*.[4] Feeling free to move
off he sailed for America by way of the South Sea and Australia. We were
packing together, they to go further east, we to come west.

NOTES

Achsah Brewster, née Barlow (1878–1945), wife of Earl Brewster: see p. 159 above.
    1. Lawrence's translation was published as *Little Novels of Sicily* (1925). He had

already translated the same author's *Mastro-Don Gesualdo*; this second translation was completed in Ceylon in March 1922.

2. Afterwards Edward VIII.

3. This poem was published in the *English Review* in April 1923 and collected in *Birds, Beasts and Flowers* in the same year. A letter written by Lawrence on 24 March 1922 contains a prose account of the same scene (*The Collected Letters of D. H. Lawrence*, ed. Harry T. Moore, II, pp. 696–7; this letter is not included in Huxley's collection).

4. This was the James Tait Black Memorial Prize, the only literary prize or award Lawrence ever received.

In Australia*

FRIEDA LAWRENCE

We arrived in Sydney harbour—nice it was not knowing a soul.

A young officer on the boat had told me: 'The rain on the tin roofs over the trenches always made me think of home.' Sydney!

And there they were, the tin roofs of Sydney and the beautiful harbour and the lovely Pacific Coast, the air so new and clean. We stayed a day or two in Sydney, two lonely birds resting a little. And then we took a train with all our trunks and said: 'We'll look out of the window and where it looks nice we'll get out.' It looked very attractive along the coast but also depressing. We were passing deserted homesteads: both in America and Australia, these human abandoned efforts make one very sad. Then we came to Thirroul, we got out at four and by six o'clock we were settled in a beautiful bungalow right on the sea. Lined with jarra the rooms were, and there were great tanks for rain water and a stretch of grass going right down to the Pacific, melting away into a pale-blue and lucid, delicately tinted sky.

But what a state the bungalow was in! A family of twelve children had stayed there before us: beds and dusty rugs all over the place, torn sailing canvases on the porches, paper all over the garden, the beautiful jarra floors grey with dust and sand, the carpet with no colour at all, just a mess, a sordid mess the whole thing. So we set to and cleaned, cleaned and cleaned as we had done so many times before in our many temporary homes! Floors polished, the carpet taken in the garden and scrubbed, the torn canvases removed. But the paper in the garden was the worst; for days and days we kept gathering paper.

* From *Not I, but the Wind*, pp. 118–21.

But I was happy: only Lawrence and I in this world. He always made a great big world for me, he gave it me whenever it was possible; whenever there was wonder left, we took it, and revelled in it.

The mornings, those sunrises over the Pacific had all the wonder of newness, of an uncreated world. Lawrence began to write *Kangaroo* and the days slipped by like dreams, but real as dreams are when they come true. The everyday life was so easy, the food brought to the house, especially the fish cart was a thrill: it let down a flap at the back and like pearls and jewels inside the cart lay the shiny fishes, all colours, all shapes, and we had to try them all.

We took long walks along the coast, lonely and remote and unborn. The weather was mild and full of life, we never got tired of the shore, finding shells for hours that the Pacific had rolled gently on to the sand.

Lawrence religiously read the *Sydney Bulletin*. He loved it for all its stories of wild animals and people's living experiences. The only papers Lawrence ever read were the *Corriere della Sera*,[1] in the past, and the *Sydney Bulletin*. I wonder whether this latter has retained the same character it had then; I haven't seen it since that time. It was our only mental food during that time.

I remember being amazed at the generosity of the people at the farms where we got butter, milk, and eggs: you asked for a pound of butter and you were given a big chunk that was nearly two pounds; you asked for two pints of milk and they gave you three; everything was lavish, like the sky and the sea and the land. We had no human contacts all these months: a strange experience: nobody bothered about us, I think.

At the library, strangely enough, in that little library of Thirroul we found several editions of Lawrence's condemned *Rainbow*.[2] We bought a copy—the librarian never knew that it was Lawrence's own book. Australia is like the 'Hinterland der Seele'.

Like a fantasy seemed the Pacific, pellucid and radiant, melting into the sky, so fresh and new always; then this primal radiance was gone one day and another primeval sea appeared. A storm was throwing the waves high into the air, they rose on the abrupt shore, high as in an enormous window. I could see strange sea-creatures thrown up from the deep: sword-fish and fantastic phenomena of undreamt deep-sea beasts I saw in those waves, frightening and never to be forgotten.

And then driving out of the tidy little town into the bush with the little pony cart. Into golden woods of mimosa we drove, or wattle, as the Australians call it. Mostly red flowers and yellow mimosa, many varieties, red and gold, met the eye, strange fern-trees, delicately leaved. We came to a wide river and followed it. It became a wide waterfall and then it disappeared into the earth. Disappeared and left us gaping. Why should it have disappeared, where had it gone?

Lawrence went on with *Kangaroo* and wove his deep underneath impressions of Australia into this novel. Thirroul itself was a new little bungalow town and the most elegant thing in it was a German gun that glistened steely and out of place there near the Pacific.

I would have liked to stay in Australia and lose myself, as it were, in this unborn country but Lawrence wanted to go to America. Mabel Dodge[3] had written us that Lawrence must come to Taos in New Mexico, that he must know the Pueblo Indians, that the Indians say that the heart of the world beats there in New Mexico.

This gave us a definite aim and we began to get ready for America, in a few weeks.

NOTES

For a note on Frieda Lawrence see p. 88.

1. A newspaper published in Milan.
2. The unexpurgated edition had been declared obscene in November 1915: the magistrate had fined the publisher and ordered that existing stocks be destroyed.
3. See p. 171.

In New Mexico*

MABEL DODGE LUHAN

We stood waiting in the sweet air, all scented as it was from the charcoal kilns burning piñon-wood. That was always the first impression of New Mexico when one got off the train at Lamy station—the thin, keen air full of a smell of incense.

Lawrence and Frieda came hurrying along the platform, she tall and full-fleshed in a suit of pale pongee, an eager look on her pink face, with green, unfocused eyes, and her half-open mouth with the lower jaw pulled a little sideways. Frieda always had a mouth rather like a gunman.

Lawrence ran with short, quick steps at her side. What did he look like to me that first time I saw him? I hardly know. I had an impression of his slim fragility beside Frieda's solidity, of a red beard that was somehow too old for him, and of a nervous incompetence. He was agitated, fussy, distraught, and giggling with nervous grimaces. Tony and I felt curiously inexpressive and stolid confronting them. Frieda was over-expansive, vociferous, with a kind of forced, false bonhomie, assumed (it felt so to me, at least) to cover her inability to strike just the real right note. As usual when there is a flurry like that, I died inside and became speechless. Tony is never any help at

* From *Lorenzo in Taos* (London: Martin Secker, 1933) pp. 44–7.

such a moment, and he just stood there. Somehow I herded them into the lunch room of the station, for we had to eat our supper there because it would be too late when we reached Santa Fé.

We got seated in a row at the counter, the atmosphere splitting and crackling all about us from the singular crash of our meeting. There was a vibratory disturbance around our neighbourhood like an upheaval in nature. I did not imagine this: it was so. The Lawrences seemed to be intensely conscious of Tony and somehow embarrassed by him. I made out, in the twinkling of an eye, that Frieda immediately saw Tony and me sexually, visualising our relationship. I experienced her swift, female measurement of him, and how the shock of acceptance made her blink. In that first moment I saw how her encounters passed through her to Lawrence—how he was keyed to her so that he felt things through her and was obliged to receive life through her, vicariously; but that he was irked by her vision; that he was impatient at being held back in the sex scale. He did not want to apprehend us so and it made him very nervous, but she was his medium, he must see through her and she had to see life from the sex centre. She endorsed or repudiated experience from that angle. She was the mother of orgasm and of the vast, lively mystery of the flesh. But no more. Frieda was complete, but limited. Lawrence, tied to her, was incomplete and limited. Like a lively lamb tied to a solid stake, he frisked and pulled in an agony, not Promethean so much as Panic.

Can it be possible that it was in that very first instant when we all came together that I sensed Lawrence's plight and that the womb in me roused to reach out to take him? I think so, for I remember thinking: 'He is through with that—he needs another kind of force to propel him...the spirit...' The womb behind the womb—the significant, extended, and transformed power that succeeds primary sex, that he was ready, long since, to receive from woman. I longed to help him with that—to be used—to be put to his purpose.

Lawrence scurried to the far seat away from us on the other side of Frieda and she and I sat next each other, with Tony beside me. The meal was an agony—a halt—an unresolved chord, for me, at least, and for Lawrence, I knew. Tony ate his supper with a calm aloofness, unperturbed in the midst of alarm. Frieda continued her noisy, running ejaculations and breathless bursts of emotional laughter. Lawrence hid behind her big body. I scarcely saw him, but we all knew he was there, all right!

As we made our way out into the dark road where the motor waited, he exclaimed:

'Oh! Look how low the stars hang in the southern sky!' It was the first simple, untroubled notice he had taken of anything since they had left the train.

When we reached the automobile, I directed him to the seat beside Tony and took Frieda into the back seat with me, though I wanted it the other way round. But I thought it was easier for Lawrence that way, and that Tony would soothe him down.

As we moved off into the still night, Frieda exclaimed loudly, motioning to Tony's wide back:

'He's wonderful! Do you feel him like a rock to lean on?'

'No—o,' I answered, hesitantly, unable to confirm her. Her words passed over to Lawrence with a thump. I saw his shoulders twitch. He did not want Frieda to think Tony was a rock to lean on; he could scarcely avoid understanding her unconscious comparison, or feeling again the old, old lack in himself. We ran smoothly on for a little while, and then, quite suddenly, the car simply stopped in the road.

'Well,' said Tony.

He got out and looked under the hood, though I well knew that, no matter what he saw, he would not understand it. He had never learned much about the motor. Only by having the car checked quite often by garage people, we rarely had any difficulty any more, though when he first learned to drive, things were always going wrong. It was extremely unusual for anything to happen as late as 1922, for Tony had been motoring about the country for four years by that time.

We sat there for ages under the stars while Tony tried different ways to make it go again. We didn't talk much. It was peaceful, but it was growing late and I had not engaged rooms anywhere in Santa Fé. The only hotel possible to stay in then had burned down and I had intended to go to a boarding-house I knew about, for the night. As we sat there, quietly, our emotions subsided, our nerves quieted. Suddenly Frieda cut in:

'Get out and see if you can't help him, Lorenzo! Just sitting there! Do get out!'

And Lawrence answered angrily:

'You know I don't know anything about automobiles, Frieda! I *hate* them! Nasty, unintelligent, unreliable things!'

'Oh, you and your hates!' she returned, contemptuously.

A moment of silence broken by a vague picking sound out in the front where Tony pried round inside the machinery. And then Lawrence leaned over from the front seat and said:

'I am a failure. I am a failure as a man in the world of men...'

Tony got into the car and tried it and it moved again.

'I guess there is some snake around here,' he said, as we drove on.

I was flustered when we reached Santa Fé. The city was sleeping. We drove to the Riches' house, where I'd hoped to find rooms, but after rousing the house we were told it was full. Lawrence had unloaded their huge bags onto the sidewalk while they waited for me to go in. Frieda had made him do that. When I came out, I found him stamping his foot in a rage and trying to yell quietly in the night at her:

'I won't do it, Frieda! You stop that...'

I interrupted him:

'We can't get in there. But I'll tell you what: Witter Bynner[1] knows you're coming. He's always up. He has room. I know he'd love to have you—and we can go to some other friends here.'

NOTES

Mabel Dodge Luhan, née Ganson (1879–1962), was a wealthy American patroness of writers and artists. Born in Buffalo, she spent some time in Europe and eventually settled in Taos, New Mexico, and in 1923 married Tony Luhan, a Pueblo Indian. She invited the Lawrences to visit her there; according to her own account, before going to sleep each night she 'leaped through space' and 'willed him to come'. Travelling from Australia via Wellington, Tahiti and San Francisco, Lawrence and Frieda arrived at Lamy, the railway station near Santa Fé, on 10 September 1922, where Mrs Luhan was waiting to meet them.

1. See p. 173.

First Impressions[*]

WITTER BYNNER

Presently the car arrived in my bleak little yard, where I had been assiduously watering downy tufts of green, still ignorant that they were tumbleweed. A red-bearded man started out of the car just as Tony decided to back it a bit, whereupon I heard my first Lawrencian explosion. He had been in Taormina, before continuing eastward round the world, and had bought there a Sicilian peasant-painting: the back panel of a cart vividly decorated with two scenes of medieval jousting. He had carried his trophy, some five feet long and two feet high, from place to place for months, his wife thinking that perhaps he would decide to settle in Taos and that there at last the panel too would rest. It never reached Taos. In my yard the panel and his mind were settled with one savage flash. The board had been under his arm as he was alighting and one end of it, being on the ground when Tony backed, had buckled and split, giving him a shove as it did so. Lawrence's thin shape cleaved air like the Eiffel Tower, his beard flamed, his eyes narrowed into hard turquoise, he dashed the panel to the earth, and his voice, rising in a fierce falsetto, concentrated on the ample woman behind him, 'It's your fault, Frieda! You've made me carry that vile thing round the world, but I'm done with it. Take it, Mr Bynner, keep it, it's yours! Put it out of my sight! Tony, you're a fool!'

* From *Journey with Genius* (New York: John Day, 1951) pp. 1–4.

Mrs Lawrence maintained a smile toward us; the Indian stirred no eyelash. Mrs Sterne, pleased with the show, took command of it by introducing us in her pleasant, innocent voice, and Lawrence shook hands with us as affably as though the outburst had not occurred. But despite Frieda's '* jas*' and noddings that she would like to keep the panel even with its crack, nobody's plea could move him to let her have it, though I believe he would have liked to keep it, too. After these many years, Mrs Lawrence still sees it on occasion in my study and laughs over its connection with our stormy first meeting.

Lawrence's appearance struck me from the outset as that of a bad baby masquerading as a good Mephistopheles. I did not feel in him the beauty which many women have felt. I have since read—in *The Savage Pilgrimage*—Catherine Carswell's[1] impressions at her first meeting with him nine years before mine. 'The immediately distinguishing thing,' she says, 'was his swift and flamelike quality . . . . I was sensible of a fine, rare beauty in Lawrence, with his deep-set jewel-like eyes, thick, dust-coloured hair, pointed underlip of notable sweetness, fine hands, and rapid but never restless movements.' Four months after that, in October, 1914, he had written her: 'I was seedy and have grown a beard. I think I look hideous, but it is so warm and complete, and such a clothing to one's nakedness, that I like it and shall keep it.' She describes it as 'a beard quite different from the hair of his head, of a deep glowing red in the sun and in the shade the colour of strong tea.' Richard Aldington[2] records, as of 1914, 'the head looks moulded of some queer-coloured stone, the beard gives the right touch of Mohammedan "touch-me-not-ye-unclean"'. I remember quickly wondering at Santa Fé in 1922 what Lawrence would look like under the beard, which gave somewhat the effect of a mask with the turquoise eyes peering from it. The beard and the hair, too, seemed like covers he was cuddling under—a weasel face hiding under the warm fur of its mother and peeking out. Mrs Carswell was accurate as to the colours. The beard, which he retained through the rest of his life, appeared to me more like a connected part of him than did his mat of hair, with its forward sidelong bang, which looked detachable, like a wig or a cap. In his writings, he forever removed that cap, exposed his cranium and its cerebral contents in all nakedness; but physically the beard clung close over his face as if he wished there the darkness into which his whole nakedness was always striving to return, or to progress. How he would have enjoyed classic proportions and a clean-cut Greek visage instead of the look of a semistarved viking! The Hon. Dorothy Brett,[3] the Taos painter from England, relates of their first meeting, 'I look up, realising with surprise the eyes are blue, not black, as I had thought.' Mrs Carswell, too, had originally thought the eyes another colour and then found them blue. Aldington recalls from his own first meeting in 1914, 'you were immediately impressed by his fiery blue eyes' which 'seemed to exist independent of their owner', whereas John Galsworthy[4] could not like the 'provincial novelist' because of his 'dead eyes'. Perhaps Lawrence could shift their colour for women. He himself, however, knew well what hue they were and how they could change in mood and temper. In *The Rainbow* he says of the Brangwens, his own clan, 'One could watch the change in their eyes from laughter to anger, blue-lit-up laughter, to a hard blue-staring anger.' Although he was to say later that all the gods have blue eyes, he had confided to Jessie Chambers ('ET'),[5] his early intimate: 'For me, a brown skin is the only beautiful one.' His own skin was too white, and I do not think he enjoyed it. Somewhere he quotes the Greeks as having said that 'a white, unsunned body was fishy and unhealthy'.

He occasionally vented in his writings his reluctant distaste for the physique he was born to carry and he tried to put the fault outside himself. Mrs Lawrence records in *Not I, but the Wind* his pathetic remark to the doctors when his end was near: 'I have had bronchitis since I was a fortnight old.' He had come through pneumonia twice in his twenties. And so when he tells, in *Kangaroo*, the bitter story of his examination and rejection for British army service, he almost blames the official for his own humiliated and unbelieving distress in not being of more heroic mould: 'The chemist-assistant puppy looked him up and down with a small grin as if to say, "Law-lummy, what a sight of a human scarecrow!"' He appeared anything but a scarecrow that evening in Santa Fé, though he was a bit gangling, and his voice was occasionally like whistlings of the wind. 'His voice,' says Aldington, 'such a pleasant devil's voice, with its shrill little titters and sharp mockeries and even more insulting flatteries. . . . I welcome his "tee-hees" and "too-hoos", which puff away a deal of silly cant and affectation.' 'A high tinkling laugh,' contributes Dorothy Brett, 'the ever-ready amused jeer.' Norman Douglas,[6] less kindly, in a comment on Lawrence's satirical writing about recognisable persons, is undoubtedly describing and disliking the physical voice: 'that squeaky suburban chuckle which is characteristic of an age of eunuchs'.

We had heard the shrillness of the Lawrence voice over the broken wagon board and we heard its variations later that evening in satirical comments on persons and places.

NOTES

Witter Bynner (1881–1968), American poet and editor, was a friend of Lawrence during his stay in New Mexico and Mexico (1922–5). His book, written nearly thirty years after the experiences described, offers a somewhat unsympathetic account of Lawrence.

1. See p. 97.
2. See p. 225.
3. See p. 201.
4. See p. 147.
5. See p. 31.
6. See p. 157, n. 1.

The Lawrences:
A Portrait *

MABEL DODGE LUHAN

I find . . . that I have given . . . no real, concrete portrait of Lawrence and Frieda. But I have here among their letters a description that a girl wrote of them, and sent to a friend and me some time during the year we were all waiting for them to come. This was a girl who had known them in England.

I think I will add this description of them, so you will be able to *see* how he looked:

Lawrence is tall, but so slightly built and so stooped that he gives the impression of a small man. His head seems too heavy for his very slim body and hangs forward. The whole expression of his figure is of extreme fragility. His movements are quick and sure. He has a very heavy crop of ash-coloured hair that is cut round in a bang and falls in sort of Greek-like locks.

In contrast to his hair, is a very soft, silky beard of bright red. He has very large, wide-apart grey eyes, a long, slender face with a chin that is out of proportion long, a defect that is concealed by the aforesaid beard. His under lip protrudes from the dainty decoration of the beard in a violent red that makes his beard look pink. In the midst of all this, is a very podgy, almost vulgar, certainly undistinguished nose. There! Can you see him? On the whole, it seems foolish to talk about Lawrence to anyone who has read his books, for he is all there, more than any other author I ever knew. *Sons and Lovers* is a fairly authentic picture of his own life. I think the events are absolutely true. His mother's death almost killed Lawrence. He had such a frightful mother complex, and still has, I fancy, that the book *had* to be written. His wife told me that when he wrote the death of his mother, she had a perfectly terrible time with him for many weeks.

But what you want to know particularly, I suppose, is what he is as a human being. He is one of the most fascinating men I ever met. The first time I ever saw him, he talked for a whole afternoon, almost steadily. He will do this at once, and without the slightest self-consciousness if he feels a

* From *Lorenzo in Taos*, pp. 48–51, 74–5.

sympathy in his listener. He talks as brilliantly as he writes, and as frankly. Have you read *Women in Love?* because that *is* Lawrence—his word. It is his final philosophy. It pours out of him like an inspired message, and no matter how much you may differ when you are away from him, or how little able you are to follow his own particular mysticism, he makes you believe it when he is with you.

But at the slightest touch of adverse criticism or hostility, Lawrence becomes violent. His vituperation is magnificent. I have never heard its equal. He spares none. He has quarrelled with everyone. He says he has no friends that he has not quarrelled with. And yet all these same friends, I noticed, are very likely to come back for the same treatment again and again. Lawrence is a Puritan, really, and his intellectual reaction against it is so violent that he hurls himself against it with all of himself, destroying himself as he does it. In the marvellously sweet side of his nature, he is inarticulate. And yet he is the gentlest, kindest person in all human relations that anyone could be on this earth. The peasants around where he lived in Cornwall adored him blindly. They looked upon him as the new Messiah come to lead the world out of the dark into a light that they couldn't understand, but which they had infinite faith in, simply because he was he.

Lawrence lives the life of a workman. He says that no matter how much money he has, he always will live just the same. I think this is true.When I visited them in Cornwall, he and his wife lived in a little stone cottage of three rooms. It was spotlessly clean, mostly done by Lawrence. All their cooking was done on an open fire in the living-room. I have even known Lawrence to do the washing, though they usually sent it out. Money means nothing to Lawrence. He is very frugal, with all the thriftiness of his working-class background, but he would share whatever he had with another without a thought. The little spotless sunny house in Cornwall had the most beautiful simplicity that I have ever seen.

His wife is a big, rosy German, who, as the daughter of a Prussian officer, never knew anything but luxury in her girlhood. She is highly impractical now, and the little she knows of housework, Lawrence taught her. She is an expansive child-nature, very sunny and rich, living only in her emotions. The story of their love life is all to be found in the poems, *Look, We Have Come Through.*[1] She is really all light and sun while Lawrence is dark; there seems to be always a weight on him. He is rarely really gay—he is truly the sombre Anglo-Saxon, which he hates with a bitter hatred.

After all, Lawrence is best known in his books, for he writes all the things he cannot say. And yet he says such a lot! But the inner tumult wears him out. He is very fragile, physically. He says that he is always well when he is happy. It is said that he has something the matter with his lungs, yet not since he was a child has a doctor ever found any actual lung trouble. When he was a little boy, I believe, his lungs were affected, but he seems to have outgrown it.

People are always making pilgrimages to him. He hates it, but is infinitely sweet to them. His awareness of other people is unbelievable. When you are with him, you feel that there is not a corner of your mind or spirit or whatever you have that Lawrence doesn't see and be tolerant of. And he bares himself perfectly frankly. When a mood or an impulse is in him, there is no such thing as repression. It all comes out in a mighty gust.

He cannot live in big cities. The excitement kills him. He is too aware all the time. The war was a horrible thing to him, came darned near killing him, through the intensity of his emotion about it.

*   *   *

We were soon leading each other into new ways. Lawrence gave great dissertations upon activity; upon *doing* things. This *doing* business has been one of the principal problems of my whole life. Nothing to do! From childhood until now I've been suffering a great deal of the time from a blank feeling that seems best-expressed in those words, and I have passed countless hours just sitting and staring straight ahead. Now, I don't believe I *ever* saw Lawrence just sit. He was forever doing something. Rather fussily, too. He did a good deal of the housework at home; he always did the baking, and at least half of the cooking and dish-washing. When Frieda and he went off together, he taught her how to do all of these things. He taught her how to wash clothes, how to scrub them clean and rinse them in cold water with blueing in it and to hang them in the sun to make them come white; and one of the few things Frieda really liked to do about the house was this washing. She always made quite an affair of it, and it usually put her in a good temper.

Lawrence really had very little sense of leisure. After the housework was done, he usually crept into a hedge or some quiet corner and wrote something, sitting on the ground with his knees drawn up. Midday brought another meal to prepare and to tidy up—and in the afternoons he made up tasks if he had none, odd jobs of carpentering or cleaning, unless he was out somewhere with us.

The only time he appeared to relax at all was at tea-time. He didn't seem to mind chatting then—and he liked his tea. But in the evenings—and we always spent them together in our house or theirs—he either delivered a monologue—a long, passionate harangue or narrative about something that he addressed to himself, his eyes not seeing us, but bent upon his inner picture, usually ending in an argument with Frieda—or else he got us all doing charades or playing some game. He loved charades—and he was so gay and witty when he was playing! He could imitate anything or anybody. His ability to identify himself intuitively with things outside himself was wonderful. We had some boisterous evenings, with Ida and Dasburg and Spud and others, that left us hot and happy and full of ease.

NOTES

For a note on Mabel Dodge Luhan see p. 171.

1. Lawrence's collection of autobiographical poems had been published in 1917; earlier titles of the collection were *Man and Woman* and *Poems of a Married Man*.

Lawrence Talking*

MAURICE LESEMANN

When I opened the door, coming in out of the blue clearness of New Mexico dusk on an October afternoon, a man stood up quickly and turned nervously toward me, looking very dark, very darkly bearded, in the firelight. But when we went in to dinner I saw that he was not so tall as I had thought, and very slight, almost frail, of body, with small shoulders and meagre arms. His head also was not large, not distinguished at all, and rather unshapely, though the reddish beard, thrusting below the chin, made it seem longer. Underneath the brow, which was wrinkled and knotted, the eyes were small and bright blue. They had weary sags beneath them. He sat as if folded in and huddled upon himself, bending over his arms, bending over his red beard. Not that he was quiet and morose—not for a moment—but I realised then, rather suddenly, what an enormous amount of writing Lawrence has done for a man of thirty-seven years, what a monstrous labour it has been, if only labour alone, without any of the desperate questioning it tells of, and the suffering.

We rode out horseback in the morning. The adobe houses of Taos were warm and golden in the sunlight as always, but now the cottonwoods and poplars too were golden for fall, and stood in thin, vibrant screens over the flat roofs and up into the blue. Out toward the Taos Pueblo the Indian fields were reaped and yellow with stubble, and the bushes by the old pueblo wagon road made a smoky mist of lavender and russet. Leaves of the wild plum trailed crimson over them. We passed Indian boys hunting birds with bows and arrows. They hid in the bushes when the ponies came close.

Lawrence was dressed in leather puttees and riding breeches; and a little white woollen coat of Scotch homespun without any collar, a strange

* From 'D. H. Lawrence in New Mexico', *The Bookman*, LIX (Mar 1924) pp. 29–32.

garment in this country, with a homely northern look about it, and underneath this, a knitted sweater that a friend had made for him of the very blue to harmonise with his red beard. He was very gay in the crisp clearness of the morning. We talked about America.

This was Lawrence's first visit to America, and he was still in the midst of first impressions. He saw our machine life as an appalling thing, a very terrible thing. It would take the most intense individualism to escape the deep-seated American impulse toward uniformity. All that a sensitive person could do now was to live totally to himself. 'He must be himself,' Lawrence said. 'He must keep to *himself* and fight against all that. There is nothing else to do. *Nothing*.'

When he talked, one forgot almost at once that first impression of frailness and weariness. One forgot the heavily knotted brow under the shock and surcharge of his eyes. He spoke gaily and whimsically. His voice was high pitched and thin, soaring high upward for emphasis, and still higher in a kind of amused exultation. Talking of uniformity, he remarked upon the way Americans treat everyone with the utmost familiarity on first acquaintance. It has become a convention with us to presume an exact community of interest. He was amazed at this. 'They tell you *all* of their affairs, and then expect *you* to tell them all of yours. They make me furious! And I know that they have the kindest intentions in the world. They mean to be kindly and generous, of course. But I have the feeling of being perpetually insulted!'

He talked of it often, the condition of American life and its possible future. He felt revolution. He felt it somehow in the peculiar mental make up of our people despite their apparent docility. There was a terrible potentiality there, a disposition to join together when aroused, a sense for joining and feeling their strength together. If I took him rightly, it was a sort of child's knowledge of the possession of power. He had an intuitive fear of them and of what they might do if ever they took a notion to overturn things, either little or great. 'I feel them dangerous,' he said, 'dangerous as a race. Far more dangerous than most of the races of Europe.'

While we talked the ponies would slacken their pace, gradually, by mutual consent, dropping at last into a slow walk, scarcely placing one foot before another. We passed the Pueblo, rising in terraces into the sun, five terraces rising with golden brown walls against the dark blue peaks of mountains behind them. The Indians were husking corn in the corrals and patios. The streets, usually swept clean as a floor, were littered with rustling husks of corn. Lawrence was always for turning out of the road and off across the fields at a gallop. He pressed his flat white hat tightly to his head and gave the little sorrel free rein, letting her go breakneck over the hardened furrows. Then back through a gap in the underbrush to the road again, the ponies excited after their run, tossing their manes.

'I should like to see the young people gather,' he said, 'somewhere away from the city, somewhere where living is cheap—in a place like this, for instance; and let them have a farm or a ranch, with horses and a cow, and *not* try to make it pay. Don't let them try to make it pay—like Brook Farm. That was the trouble with Brook Farm. But let them support themselves by their writing, or their painting, or whatever it is.' I had been telling him of the large number of young people in America who are intent on creative work in the arts and are up against the kaleidoscopic, emotionally disintegrating life of our commercial centres. He came back again and again to this increasing problem of preserving the individual entity. 'They could be *themselves* there,' he said, 'and they would form a nucleus. Then they would be able gradually to spread their influence and combat the other thing a little. At least they would know they existed...'

'At any rate, it would be an interesting experiment.'

And with the last words off he would go, urging the little mare into a lope and standing up in the stirrups. He pressed the small white hat tightly to his head and sat far forward in the saddle, leaning over eagerly. He rode eagerly. The white coat flapped behind him in the wind.

This eagerness and exultation were constant in him. One night by the fire he told stories about English people he had known, imitating with absurd nicety their voices and manner, their entire conversation. He described their way of walking, and must needs jump from his chair and pace up and down the floor—yes, all round the room, taking the part first of the Countess and then of the Cabinet Minister—until finally they rose before us—heroic, monumental in caricature. And then Lawrence would remember one thing more, and it so ridiculous that he would have to sit down; and his voice would break and go careering away into a chuckling laugh before he could tell what had overpowered him....

Sometimes, of course, the eagerness and the exultation were more concentrated within him, and there was less of them for the rest of us. Sometimes he was altogether inward, as if there were an actual physical change in him, a periodic withdrawal of his energies deep inside him. At such a time his remarks in criticism of people were very piercing. Very quick, darting out at them and back again. And his voice was a bit aside from us, and a bit wary; sharp, at a moment. And his eyes too were sharp, darting askance. It was almost as if he were at a distance from us in the room, conversing in his high voice at a short but distinct distance, as if he were sitting quite by himself over there beyond the table, under the small shine of the candles.

On such an evening one felt him strangely in the house. Although he talked, and talked gaily and whimsically, yet he himself was present otherwise, in some totally different way. He had an exquisite, almost physical sensitiveness to the personalities about him. Like Cicio in *The Lost Girl*, and others of his most authentic characters—those who are least explained—he became then an enigmatic intuitive being: irritated darkly within by the slightest contacts, feeling them to the point of pain, or stirred with delight in the same mordant fashion, but never ceasing, never relenting. The small blue eyes burned and danced, indestructible. He penetrated the room and its peculiar atmosphere with excruciating understanding.

'If you fall from the tower of a cathedral and your mind says that you shall die, you will *die*; and if your mind is not going to die then, you will *not* die.' And I shall always remember his casual remark. For him it is true. His mind must go on without rest, creating beyond itself, thrusting out beyond itself again and again in flashes of vision.

NOTE

Lesemann, a minor American poet, visited Lawrence in Taos in October 1922.

In Mexico *

WITTER BYNNER

Interested in the Indian revival which was being encouraged by the Minister of Education, with men like Dr Atl renouncing their Spanish names in favour of Aztec, Lawrence expressed one evening a desire to meet Sr Vasconcelos;[1] and Leighton[2] arranged for us all to have lunch with the Minister and Carleton Beals.[3]

When we had assembled in the waiting room, a sudden complication had arisen, and a polite request was sent us that our appointment might be postponed till the following day.

Lawrence went stiff. He blanched. Then he sprang to his feet, crying 'I'm busy too! I won't meet the man! Tell him I won't meet him!' Hysteria fed itself. He began denouncing not only Vasconcelos, but the government and finally the whole Mexican race.

His mate made matters worse by saying, 'Men of importance have unforeseen interruptions, Lorenzo.'

'I'm important too!' His voice cut the air like a saw. 'But I don't break engagements at the last moment! Frieda, you're an imbecile!'

Leighton and Johnson[4] were held quiet, bewildered; but I was irritated and put in another mistaken word, 'What's one more day in Mexico? Besides, it was we who wanted to meet him, not he who wanted to meet us.'

'I was a dolt to want to meet him,' he shrilled, 'and we'll have an end of

* From *Journey with Genius*, pp. 26–8, 37–9, 48–52, 54–5, 110–12, 341–3.

it. Just tell him, Leighton, that I refuse to meet an impertinent political puppy!'

Leighton and Beals left in one direction, we in another.

On the walk back to the hotel, Lawrence, his temper vented, chuckled at us, 'Before you joined us in Mexico, I was asked to meet one of President Obregon's secretaries at the British Consulate. The Secretary handed me a telegram that had been sent to the President: "I am America's most important author," it said. "I have come to your country to put it on the map, as I put Cuba on the map. But I wish co-operation. I wish at my disposal an automobile and chauffeur, a private railway car, and for companion and guide an official who speaks English." "Is he so important?" the Secretary asked me. "No," I said. "He's a third-rate American novelist. Don't answer him." And the fellow got no reply. But I wish now,' snapped Lawrence, 'that I'd suggested Vasconcelos for "companion and guide". They'd have deserved each other.'

'It was Booth Tarkington,'[5] added Mrs Lawrence brightly.

'Nothing of the sort, you silly gabbler,' he retorted. 'What do you ever get straight? It was Joseph Hergesheimer.'[6]

A bit in *Sons and Lovers* throws light on Lawrence's frenzy toward Vasconcelos. Of himself he says, 'He was the sort of boy that becomes a clown and a lout as soon as he is not understood, or feels himself held cheap.' In *The Lost Girl* he had written: 'If a man is conscious of being a *gentleman*, he is bound to be a little less than a *man*. . . . If a man must loftily, by his manner, assert that he is *now* a gentleman, he shows himself a clown.' It is odd that such self-knowledge did not more comfortably direct its possessor's conduct.

That night, from our room next door to theirs, Johnson and I could hear his voice scaling higher and higher as he berated his wife for the sins of Vasconcelos and the world. 'Such a pleasant devil's voice,' says Aldington. But the devil was not pleasant this night. It is an odd phenomenon in my experience that time and time again, a marked exception being Norman Douglas, English men of letters have these treble, almost soprano, voices. Lytton Strachey's and E. M. Forster's are famous. Lawrence's normal tone was high enough; but when he was agitated it would lift its pitch and then the sound of the rise would further excite it till it was as high as it could go. Wave after wave of fifelike fury dashed on Mrs Lawrence. I myself by this time had been alternately fevered and chilled with anger toward Lawrence and was determined that, even though he changed his mind, he was not to be allowed a meeting with Vasconcelos but that we were to take her with us, come what may. It was not a question of allowing. He stood firm. He would not go. At least in our presence, he raised no objection to his wife's accompanying us and she made next day a plausible apology for his absence, pleading illness. Sr Vasconcelos proved to be cordial, interesting, generous, anything but a 'puppy'. 'An unordinary man,' nodded Frieda, 'just the sort you should meet, Lorenzo.' But they never

met. It is recorded that to the inspector of the school at Croydon Lawrence
in his youth had never said, 'Sir'.

*   *   *

After Puebla, we went to Orizaba. It seems to me that our trip was by night
and that we arrived there not very well rested and pinched with an early
morning chill. There was at any rate a definite chill in ourselves as soon as
we set foot on the platform. Lorenzo, with his cold worse, with a hard face,
and with nervous jerks of his head in this and that direction, waved porters
aside and suddenly walking between them and us, ejaculated with the now
too familiar high pitch of a nervous seizure: 'We are not staying here,
Frieda. We are leaving.' He inquired the hour of the next train back.
Frieda gave a sigh of relief when we learned that it was considerably later.
She asked him what the matter was. 'Don't you feel it?' he railed. 'Don't
you feel it through your feet? It exudes from the platform. The place is evil.
I won't go to the town, I won't go to a hotel, I won't go anywhere. I can
stay here at the station till train time. You can do as you like. The place is
evil, the whole air is evil! The air creeps with it!' And he screamed at the
finally intimidated porters to go away.

   My patience broke. I tried hard to speak quietly and perhaps did.
'Lorenzo, I am going to see the town. If I like it I am going to spend the
night. There is no reason why I should give in to your whims. I knew from
the way you treated Leighton that I ought not to come with you and I'm
sorry now that I did. But you're not going to boss me. I'm going to the
hotel. If Frieda wants to come along, you can indulge your nerves here by
yourself.' I don't know whether or not my voice shook from the shaking of
my ganglion.

   He looked extremely and childishly surprised, not as if my standing him
off was a shock, but as if it was an unwarranted attack on him out of the
blue. He was instantly docile and dumb. He followed us into the vehicle.
He sank his beard into his breastbone. He was a deflated prophet.

   And then came in my own history one of its most comic episodes. We
reached a friendly old-fashioned Mexican hotel, built around a court, the
two-story arched patio lined with potted plants and flowers, the walls hung
with caged birds, the rooms sequestered in the old Mexican way so that
when room doors were closed there would be darkness and no air, the
dining room with its soiled tablecloths, and the kitchen with its charcoal
stoves open amiably to the sociable pigskin chairs on the ground floor. All
was as it should be for the native or the open-minded foreign guest. I liked
it and was tired and was glad to see my suitcase at rest in a corner. But the
devil entered me. I waited until the Lawrences might have unpacked some
of their belongings and be relaxing. Then I knocked at their door. Frieda
opened it. I stalked in. 'It's impossible,' said I. 'There must be another
hotel. I can't stay here.'

'Why not?' asked Lorenzo, a pathetic martinet.

'Why not?' I yelled. 'I couldn't close an eye here. The whole atmosphere is polluted. Evil seeps up from the ground under the whole building, nothing but evil. We must leave and leave now.'

'You think the hotel is evil too? You think it's that bad?' asked Lawrence, with the eyes of an alarmed child.

'Think?' I stormed. 'I know. Don't you feel it in your feet? It comes up from the floors. I'll find another hotel. Stay if you like, but I'm leaving.'

'We'll go with you,' peeped Lawrence. 'Only a few minutes to pack.' He was utterly meek.

We cancelled our rooms. The hotel boys, thinking us maniacs because of my storming, carried our luggage to an inferior hotel two squares away. I went ahead, saw two rooms, chose for the Lawrences an airless enclosure alongside the noisome hotel privy, returned to the lobby and led them to their miserable quarters—mine were miserable too—orating, 'This is better. We are away from that poison. This is safe. This is decent. We can sleep.'

*   *   *

Lawrence had heard in Europe high praise of the famous Spanish matadors, Belmonte and Joselito, the latter killed in the ring only three years before; and we were told that the Mexicans, Rodolfo Gaona and Juan Silveti, were performers of comparable skill and prowess. Silveti was to be the star on Sunday.

On Easter morning [1923], having been to church Friday and to a sacred movie on Saturday, we were wakened by bells of resurrection and in the afternoon attended the bullfight.[7] It was a first experience for all of us, and we approached it curious but apprehensive.

At the entrance to the arena Lawrence, Johnson, and I, like other males filing through, were frisked for firearms: it had been announced that President Obregón would be present. At the last moment, word spread that he could not attend; but other dignitaries entered the presidential box escorting three or four bright-fluttering women who wore flowered mantillas and high combs.

Since seats cost but half as much in the sun as in the shade, we were sitting in the sun, except that this day, to Lawrence's special pleasure, there was no sun. Our backless bench tier of concrete was within five rows of the ring. Below us, paralleling the wall of the ring was a circling five-foot wooden fence with here and there a gap and before each gap a small barrier, making safety boxes for performers when hard pressed. The crowd, now thickening and seeming less an assemblage than a single mass monster, was already—with its murmurs, growls, and yells—grinding our nerves a little.

'I begin to feel sick,' whispered Lawrence. 'Look at their faces. The eyes don't seem hard, or the mouths. It's that cruel dent of relish above the nostril.'

Opposite us, rose a roar of voices. Somebody's hat had been tossed across the tiers into a group which was scrambling for it. Other hats followed, on our side too. Orange peels began flying. A shoe landed in Lawrence's lap. He sat immobile while someone from behind him seized it and sent it scaling again.

'Shall we leave?' asked Lawrence, his head twitching upward like that of a horse.

Half an orange just missed my bald spot. A second half hit it. Other bare heads were being hit. A kindly Mexican motioned that I should put on my hat. Obeying him, I was spared further pelting. Apparently uncovered heads were permissible targets.

Three bands, one at a time, entered their sections near the President's box and were shouted at for *musica*! When a rousing Mexican march blared out, the vocal din was only accelerated. The crowd had not wanted music so much as a beat for their own noise.

What looked like a folded coat landed in the arena. It seemed a signal. Like water from a broken dam, the mass of men in unreserved seats swelled over the reserved section which in a trice was filled solid. Seat-holders who came later were vain claimants.

On the exact moment advertised, a wide gate opened, a square colourful procession strutted with music into the arena toward the President's box to make bows, with waists and trim buttocks held tautly, shoulders back; two groups of fine-stepping *toreros* with bright cloaks above their embroidered boleros and half-length, skin-tight trousers and salmon-coloured stockings; then mounted picadors; then *banderilleros* with silver embroidery; then matadors with gold and with red capes, all these men wearing berets over abbreviated pigtails; and finally, in red harness, two dingy teams of three mules each, ready to drag away carcasses. 'The right symbol!' muttered Lawrence. 'They're all jackasses.' The procession, after circling the ring and receiving a round of plaudits, dispersed.

Then, with no warning, no noise, a huge white bull swam into the arena and stood a moment, his tail waving, his head bewildered, apprehending foes. Lawrence's head rose and sank with the bull's. 'The bull is beautiful, Lorenzo,' said Frieda. The foes were there, the first of them: two stationary horsemen. When the lowered head made clumsily for a horse, the rider warded it off with a lance. The second rider did likewise. And then into the ring came the *toreros*, to nag him with scarlet mantles. He saw them one at a time. He snorted. He charged a cloak. It was whisked over his head. He curved quickly and charged again, cleaving the air with his horns under a swing of colour. Now and then he would corner a *torero* who, amid jeers and whistlings, would either dodge into one of the safety boxes or vault the *barrera* into the shielded alley way. All of a sudden the bull too had heaved his pawing bulk over the fence. Attendants scurried to cut off a section of the gangway by closing gates. Commotion subsided. 'He beat them,' Lawrence said as though to himself. 'They should let him go.' A fluttered cape teased the bull out again into the ring, where he stood still, waving his tail. His belly lifting, falling with his heavy breath, he looked round and lowed; then once more he leaped the fence, this time breaking it. And once more the blocked exit, once more the flashing taunts, the deft weavings and wavings of five *toreros*; once more his return to the ring, his half-seeing eye, his wasted strength. 'They're dastardly!' Lawrence exclaimed.

He turned to us. He had been shifting in his seat and looking sharply at us now and then as if to see what we thought of it all. We could tell that the teasing of the beast, the deliberate baiting and angering had made him as tense as the animal, with whom he was almost identifying himself. 'They keep him starved and in the dark,' he snapped, 'so that when he comes into the ring he's angry but can't see. He's the only one among them with heart or brain. He despises them, but he knows what they are; he knows that he's done for.' The toreador jumped the fence to get away from the bull; the bull jumped the fence to get away from the lot of them. 'They let the toreador get away. Why don't they let the bull get away?' he exhorted us. 'Why don't they respect his intelligence and bow to him instead of to those nincompoops in the box? He's not the brute; they're the brutes. He abhors them and so do I. But he can't get away and I can. Let's get away.' He was on his feet. None of us stirred to follow him. He sat down again.

'It sickens me too, Lorenzo,' I agreed. 'But hadn't we better see at least one round of it through, to know what we're talking about when we say we don't like it? I shan't want to see another bullfight any more than you will.'

'Very well,' he glared. 'But I don't need to see a round through, as you call it. The trouble is that you're as bloodthirsty as the rest of them. You can't resist it. Frieda can't resist it. Spud can't. I could resist it, but I'll give in to you.' He sulked back on the bench and looked away from us, away from everything.

But now came a change, a chance for the bull to vent his disgust, if not on a man, then on a decrepit, blindfolded horse. The rider spurred toward him. The picador, with armour under his trousers, urged the shivering mount to expose its belly. The crowd was hushed, expectant, on the edge of its seats. Lawrence was breathing hard and glaring. Suddenly, given a chance not so much by the rider as by the bull, the horse struck with his thin hind legs, fought free and stalked off with an air of doddering valour, only to postpone a next encounter not at the centre of the ring where he had had clearance, but close to the *barrera*, with no room for him to dodge; and though the picador was supposed with his blunt lance to shunt the bull off, the crowd knew better. The bull pawed up earth, slowly bent his head. The lance was futile. The horse reared and floundered. In and up went the horn. While the picador tumbled against the fence and sheepishly found his feet, the bull shoved and gored and ripped; and while the crowd gave a sigh of relief, Lawrence groaned and shook. By the time the *toreros* had again drawn their prey toward the cloaks and the picador had remounted and forced his steed into motion toward the exit, the horse's bowels were bulging almost to the ground, like vines and gourds. But the bull had not had enough. 'Stop it!' cried Lawrence to the bull, jumping out of his seat. But just before the picador reached the gate, horns were lowered again for another snorting plunge, and this time the entire covering of the horse's belly was ripped off. He fell dead, his contents out on the ground, with earth being shovelled over them by attendants. Lawrence had sat down again, dazed and dark with anger and shame. Frieda was watching him. The proud front of the bull—head, neck, chest, leg, hoof—shone crimson in a moment of sun. The crowd was throatily satisfied!

There had been something phallic, Lawrence might have noted, in this fierce penetration, this rape of entrails, this bloody glut. But his nerves exploded. Fortunately people were too intent on the ring to notice him, and only a few of them heard a red-bearded Englishman, risen from his seat, excoriating cowards and madmen. Frieda was as alarmed as Johnson and I, for he was denouncing the crowd in Spanish. But he sickened suddenly, plunged away from us, treading toes, and lurched down the row toward the exit.

'I'll go with him,' exclaimed Frieda. 'I'd better. There's no knowing. You stay. He'll be worse if you come. You stay. Leave him to me. *Ja!*' And she squeezed her way out. . . .

Lawrence greeted me at the hotel with a hard look of contempt. 'So you stayed through all of it. I thought you would. You Americans would run to any street accident to see blood. You are as bad as the dirty Mexicans. You would have held Frieda there in that slaughterhouse. You tried to keep her there.'

'No, Lorenzo!' she protested.

'But they wanted you to stay. I know. They not only fooled themselves with their nonsense about "seeing it through", they wanted to fool you as well, but you were too fine for them.'

'He compliments me,' smiled Frieda. 'How angry he must be with you!'

At supper, after Johnson's return from the bullfighter's hotel, Lawrence expatiated. 'What we saw this afternoon,' he snorted, 'was the grandeur of Rome, soiling its breeches! You like scatological jokes, Bynner. No wonder you liked this dirt.'

'He didn't like it,' Spud defended me mildly, 'any more than I did.'

'You both stayed it through,' flamed Lawrence. 'The way not to enjoy it was not to stay it through.'

The Pole was with his friend at a nearby table and, when they had finished eating, came over to ours and asked if they might join us. But before bringing the Mexican, he touched off the fuse. 'It was my sixth bullfight,' he gloated. 'I was shocked at first, like you, Mrs Lawrence. I saw that Mr Lawrence had to take you out. But I've learned now. Didn't you see how happy the bulls were?' He beckoned to the Mexican and continued, 'I'd like to have you meet my—'

'No,' said Lawrence firmly. 'I do not wish to meet your friend, or anyone else in this loathsome country. And I have seen, as well, all that I wish to see of you.'

'*Ja!*' nodded Frieda vigorously.

The Pole was silenced. But as most Mexicans react when bullfights are condemned, the friend was kindled and, more because Lawrence had left the ring than because of this rudeness, he came close and took up the cudgels. 'You are English,' he challenged in our tongue. 'You run after animals, little foxes, tire them out and then let dogs tear them to pieces, while you ride your high horses. We Mexicans face big animals, stronger than we are, and we are not dogs. We face them as men and kill them with our hands. You English hunt little people too and make dogs of your soldiers to tear little people to pieces.'

'I abominate fox hunts,' sparred Lawrence, in confusion.

But the Mexican did not spare him. 'You have judged all Mexico by one bullfight, but I will not judge all England by one Englishman.' He bowed to Frieda, turned on his heel and conducted the Pole with him out of the dining room, out of the hotel.

By now Lawrence was seething, and I expected further outbursts against one or all of us. To my surprise the seething settled; and, with no more mention of Poles or Mexicans, we had a pacific session in their room, during which he opened one of those stores of information with which he frequently surprised us. He had been studying somewhere the history of bullfighting and had taken notes, in fact he produced a page of data and he half read, half remembered for us:

'In the sixteenth century the Vatican took a stand against the filthy business, which was going on here even then. Pope Pius V,' he glanced at a note, 'banned it. So did Sixtus V. But a great protest followed, led by poets,' he gave me a look, 'and by the whole faculty at Salamanca. With the next Pope,' and here a final use of the paper, 'yes, Clement VIII, the Church gave in, just as it had to give in to your Penitentes in New Mexico and to letting your Indians add their pagan rites to the Mass. That was different. I like that. I suppose a Church which murdered heretics shouldn't mind the murder of a few bulls.' He dropped the sheet of notes into a wastebasket and smiled indulgently when I picked them out again.

*   *   *

Daily Lawrence would accompany Frieda from their house to the beach and would then stroll along the sand or sit on the terrace while the three of us bathed or chatted at the water's edge. They would arrive together, he in shirt and trousers, she in bathing clothes and bath wrap. It occurred to Spud that it would be easier if she used one of our rooms for changing. This would save her having to walk home sometimes with the bathrobe over chilly wetness. She liked the idea and Lorenzo nodded. So for several weeks it was daily custom that she shift clothes in Spud's room while he and I used mine. Lorenzo then discontinued coming with her. I judged that he had thought it more seemly to accompany her when she walked through the streets in her bathrobe but that now, since she came and went conventionally clothed, she did not need escort. We all felt, moreover, that he was glad of extra hours for his writing which had begun in earnest; and we knew well by this time that the beach was not his happy terrain.

During the third week, he followed along one day an hour behind Frieda, and it happened to be a time when most of our young friends were romping in the lake with us, the usual games, the shoulder divings forward or backward with newly learned somersaults, the races, the swimming between legs with occasional heaves from underwater and more somersaults. Frieda would give buoyant approbation, sometimes clapping her hands, but never participated in the games. Lawrence was now watching with visible disapproval. If she had been looking at him, she might have let loose one of her verbal bolts and scotched him. Spud called my attention to him. He stood staring like an angry schoolmaster, his red beard stuck out toward us accusingly. Nor did he stir for some ten or fifteen minutes but waited till our bathing was ended for the day and we came ashore.

Fortunately none of the Mexicans near us, young or old, knew English.

'Why do you act like this?' he rasped at Spud and me. 'Making idiots of yourselves with all these little fools! It isn't dignified and what's more it's dangerous.'

'D-dangerous?' we stammered.

'Yes, dangerous! Don't you realise how dirty these little chits are? They begin early down here doing everything. And you let them shin up on your shoulders and clutch you round the neck and rub their dirt into you. You don't know what diseases they have, what you might catch. It's outrageous, it's reckless, and it's a silly spectacle. People are talking.'

Frieda failed us this time. She had been taken as unaware as we. She did boom, 'Lorenzo!!' But that was all. The boys knew that something was wrong and waded offshore.

As for ourselves, we were surprised but not dumb. 'Enough of that, Lawrence' was my hot retort. 'You can yell at Frieda if she'll take it. But you can't yell at me. I won't take it and you'd better find that out. Good night.'

Spud followed me into the hotel. When we reached the terrace, I remembered Frieda. We looked back. She had not moved but was standing like Lot's wife. Suddenly Lawrence seized her arm and she swayed off beside him, wet and unwilling. Each time she pulled back, he jerked her forward.

We sent her clothes along after them by Ysidoro, one of the boys he had lambasted.

Next afternoon when they came to the beach, Frieda was already in her bathing clothes. They joined us in some beach chairs.

'Lorenzo prefers that I dress at home,' she remarked, with a slight edge of relish. 'He's being considerate. He thinks I'm a nuisance to you.'

'A nuisance?' wondered Spud.

'No, he doesn't,' I twitted. 'You're not being considerate, Lorenzo. That's not it.'

'I'm not considerate at all,' he flared. 'But I don't like her dressing there and she's not going to dress there.'

'If it's convenient for her,' I retorted, still smarting from his lecture of the day before, 'she's the one you might be thinking of.'

He seemed to take no offence but turned his beard toward others around us and then toward us and hesitantly, as if afraid of his own remark but unable to restrain it, whispered the strangest sentence I ever heard from him, 'It's not a question of being considerate of any of you. It's what people will think.'

Frieda gave a deep sigh, then suddenly laughed and so did Spud. Too disgusted to laugh, I tried to down a new ground swell of dislike for the man by what I thought a friendly gesture. 'Mr Scott and his daughter want to see something of you and Frieda and I think you'd find him interesting. Why don't you join us all for supper tonight?'

I doubted, from his grimace toward Frieda, if he wished to accept. He apparently had not found the Scotts interesting; but when Frieda said, 'Gladly we'll come, not tonight, tomorrow,' he did not demur.

We sat at a table and lapsed into silence, while the sunset became radiance through which at any moment the hand of Michaelangelo's God might have reached to touch our fingers and set them busy again about small matters, touched our minds too and set them busy again about such small questions as 'What will people think?'

*   *   *

'Au revoir,' he had written, but I was certain that I should not see him again. Over the page of his letter, as over the face of a stricken person, I had felt the cast of dissolution. The spirit of the phoenix was still there; but, despite his yearnings for return to New Mexico, his promise of return must have been known in his heart as a mirage. His body was caught in the Europe he had abjured. I should not be seeing him.

So I began still again to remember the man. I remembered him that first night at my house when he split the painted piece of Sicilian cart and flew into a rage. I remembered him genial at the corner table in the Monte Carlo; silhouetted slim and active on a pyramid at Teotihuacan; crisping the station platform at Orizaba with his dark heat; striking at the bullfight with his fist, at Frieda with his forked tongue, at Leighton with his icy eye, at me through the orphans in Chapala.

I could not remember his clothes, whereas Frieda's were always hung like solid fleecy clouds around her, almost as though she were carrying a lamb; but I would remember, under whatever he wore, the bony white body which I once saw bobbing in the water of the inlet near his Chapala house. I remembered his kind keen fingers in the yarn of the serape at the hospital and the little silver tokens he had given me to string. And the letters afterward, impatient against all deadness: manly, alert, fired with final fairness and decency, the cold loneness relenting into friendship. I remembered his going back twice to Mexico, toward which he had been like a dog hurt without knowing why. Mexico had punished him; and yet he was a Pipsy drawn back to Mexico, wondering with hurt eyes. But New Mexico was different. 'Anyhow in New Mexico, the sun and the air are alive, let man be what he may.' The sun and the air were alive still, and perhaps that was enough for him to know, even though he alive could not quite reach them. Perhaps he had done enough for man. Man might now shift for himself.

While I remembered, from our days in Mexico, each trivial petulance, each whale of a whim, each self-importance, each flaming intolerant outbreak, I remembered also the lost-child look, the wistful wandering, the earnest hope, the quest, the quickening fire, the essential fundamental generosity toward both the individual and mankind. He would not have berated too much, if he had not expected too much and cared too much; and as often as not he was castigating, in the image of another, himself. My distaste for his doctrinal balancing of love with hate, of peace with war, of faultless hero with blind adherent, was melted into understanding of his fundamental, ultimate zeal to find some explanation of life—an explanation which would not be aerated philosophy, or idealisation away from facts, but would meet facts head on, would face both the animal in man and the man in animal, would face them with intrepid determination to wring out of life and death everything good and true that he could find in them. In the depth of him, he would not sentimentalise, he would not falsify or avoid, he would not fabricate or fancify, he would find out all he could by observation, by contemplation, by practice, by honesty of body and spirit; and, though in the end the struggle might be unavailing and death conquer him, his fate would be the fate of good men before and after him, and he would have had all he could have of integrity. Meantime if there were any course in thought or emotion by which death might be explained as an intelligible part of life, he would find that course. I began to feel that his lifelong fleeing from place to place, from person to person, from emotion to emotion, from idea to idea, had been in reality a perpetual flight from death itself. He. had long known that he was ill, with a likelihood of short span ahead. Had he always been haunted by death? Was that why he had worked at such a high-fever pitch? Was death what he had been trying to hide from when he fled over sea and land, hoping for a while that death might not follow? In *The Man Who Died*, he wrote of the tired Christ, seeing life again with the eyes of death: 'It was fear, the ultimate fear of death that made men mad. So always if he stayed, his

neighbours wound the strangling of their *fear* and bullying round him.'
Was that why Lawrence wandered? Or had he been fleeing his own fear of
death? Or had he been hunting to find death and its meaning before death
should stop him? Had he been less a fugitive than a hunter? Whatever the
case, I discovered myself—as I felt his image sitting under the willow tree
on the beach, near the burros or walking a hill in the dusk—more and more
at peace with him.

NOTES

For a note on Witter Bynner see p. 173. Accompanied by Bynner and his friend
Willard Johnson (see below, n. 4), the Lawrences visited Mexico City and other
parts of Mexico early in 1923. During this time Lawrence began to write *The
Plumed Serpent*.

1. José Vasconcelos, Mexican academic and politician, head of the National
University of Mexico and Minister of Education at the time Lawrence was in
Mexico City.

2. Frederic W. Leighton, American resident in Mexico City and friend of
Bynner, acted as a guide to the Lawrences.

3. American journalist and author; he was at this time teaching in Mexico City.

4. Willard Johnson (nicknamed 'Spud'), American writer, edited the magazine
Laughing Horse, to which Lawrence contributed.

5. Booth Tarkington (1869–1964), American novelist.

6. Joseph Hergesheimer (1880–1924), American novelist.

7. This account may be compared with the opening chapter of *The Plumed
Serpent*.

The Café Royal Episode*

CATHERINE CARSWELL

If I could help it, I would never intrude upon Lawrence when Murry was
there—and Murry frequently was there—because I could not bear the
underlying sense of strain and dissatisfaction. Frieda was torn between her
recent friendliness with Murry and Lawrence's belief that England held
nothing for him any more in spite of all the *Adelphis*[1] that were or ever could
be. Lawrence, waiting in vain week after week for some reply to the letters
and cables which he was sending to his New York publisher, had begun to
be anxious about money. Where was the use of his books going well in the

* From *The Savage Pilgrimage*, pp. 214–24.

States if he received nothing for them?' 'It was a painful time,' says Murry. So it was.

Of the 'painful things that happened in it' I was certainly witness to one. But on that occasion the special painfulness was created by Murry. Possibly from a conscious desire that Lawrence should be spared, he has not told the story in his *Reminiscences*.[2] It has since been given, however, from hearsay and with the most circumstantial inaccuracy by Mrs Luhan. As the incident concerned neither Lawrence nor Murry alone, but inclusively nine of us, it seems imperative that it should be given here correctly to the best of my remembrance.

During this visit of Lawrence to London he was determined to make at least one attempt at friendly gaiety—a sort of 'Well, well, now that we are here don't let's be too gloomy even if we have made a mistake' gesture on his part. He went with Koteliansky[3] to the Café Royal, engaged a private room there and ordered a supper. (For which, to Lawrence's annoyance, the manager insisted upon having a deposit, and refused to take a cheque.) When Frieda first told me that they were giving a party in a restaurant, I took it merely as an announcement, not as an invitation. I knew that Lawrence had a considerable acquaintance in London, and it struck me as natural that we, living in the same house and seeing each other constantly, were not to be among the guests. But when I said I hoped they would have a good evening, Frieda shouted in amazement: 'But you and Don[4] are coming! You are *invited*! It is a dinner for Lawrence's friends!'

Only then did I recognise my half-unconscious withdrawal on the first reception of the news, as a too willing abnegation. From the first I had felt a slight sinking of the heart at the notion of this supper, so far as I might have any part in it. And it was this that made me utter a feeble and ill-mannered protest even thus late. 'Are you quite sure that you want us?' I asked. 'There are so many people you must want to see and we can eat together any night.' 'No, no,' sang Frieda, quite shocked and hurt, I could see. 'This is for Lawrence's real friends. Are you not his real friends?' So it was settled. It was just the presence of some of those other 'real friends' that was saddening to me in the prospect. But we had to enter into the spirit of the thing, and attend with goodwill this, the one and only formal gathering I have ever known Lawrence to initiate.

Soon enough we knew who the others were to be—Koteliansky, Murry and Mark Gertler[5] for the men; Mary Cannan[6] and Dorothy Brett[7] for the women. The round table was attractively laid and the room intimate. Lawrence made a charming host—easy, simple and warm. There was something at once piquant and touching in seeing him receiving us, his friends, thus in surroundings so unlike those in which we had been accustomed to forgather with him these ten years past. It emphasised the lack of sophistication in him which, combined with his subtlety, was so moving a charm. 'Schoolboyish' is perhaps the last adjective that could justly be applied to this mature and refined, this disciplined and impassioned artist, that was D. H. Lawrence at the age of thirty-nine. But at any moment, surroundings like the Café Royal, or the rooms of some fine old house not in the cottage style, would bring out in Lawrence a boyishness that was as comic as it was lovable. 'You'll see I'm quite up to this,' he seemed to be saying. 'Mind you play up to me, so that nobody will have the slightest idea that we don't dine in marble halls all the year round.' It is never a thing to underline, but it *is* a thing to be remembered, that Lawrence was the son of a miner and spent his youth in a miners' row—no matter with how superior a mother or how sensitive a group of brothers and sisters. For him, for instance, to visit at a house like Garsington Manor,[8] was a genuine experience. He coped with it admirably and he knew just what estimation to put upon it, both as an experience and as a phenomenon. He could add up the life behind it and 'see through' the persons belonging to it, without being in any way dazzled or shaken. Even the utmost of kindly patronage could not keep him from the eventual expression of his summing up. More even than Robert Burns in his adventures with the rich and the famous, Lawrence was the 'chiel amang them takin' notes'.[9] Yet he never became sophisticated enough not to be superficially over-impressed at the first impact with personages like the Meynell family[10] or Bertrand Russell[11] or Lady Ottoline Morrell. With them this most un-schoolboyish man betrayed a kind of quiet school-boy knowingness that is not unrelated to nervousness. And the reaction from his impressibility (as in the case of Robert Burns) was apt to be violent. People gave themselves away to Lawrence in an extraordinary degree. And as often as not, their 'giving away' was a subtle form of patronage, a fact that was by no means lost on the observer and writer of fiction who lurked with cool eyes behind the poet in Lawrence. It was naturally a shock when, out of what had seemed a pleasant friendship, there should spring such prodigies, at once fantastic and recognisable, as figure in certain of his novels and tales. True, he did this with any or all of us. But one cannot escape from the touch of malice in certain instances, nor from the belief that it is there as a make-weight for the special sensibility of a man whose genius has lifted him out of his class.

To return to the Café Royal. Frieda, as our hostess, purred loudly and pleasantly. Cafés Royal or Tudor houses were not even child's play to her! She wore, greatly to Lawrence's approval, something that was both gleaming and flower-like—anyhow petal-like, as she delightedly pointed out. I forget how Dorothy Brett was dressed, except that what she wore seemed tame beside Frieda's gaiety. Mary in *décolletée* black, with a large picture hat, *à la* Mrs Siddons, looked like the heroine from a forgotten novel by John Oliver Hobbes.[12] I, too, was in black—velvet to Mary's silk. The men wore their everyday clothes. Kot, in his dark clothes as ever, looked both the most conventional and the strangest.

The food was excellent, but somehow the feast did not go well. Gertler was silent and looked watchful, even contemptuous. Kot conceived a murderous dislike for Donald, next to whom he was placed. Mary had nothing to say. I too was stricken with dumbness. Lawrence did his best to enliven us all with wine, bidding us to drink our fill and rejoice in a festive occasion. He set us a good example and drank level. There was *no* champagne. We drank claret. And never before, nor since, have I swallowed so many glasses and remained so heavily sober. With the coming of the dessert a mistake was made. What was the wine to be? asked Lawrence. Murry and Donald both said port. They had forgotten, or had not known, that port was a drink Lawrence could not well tolerate. He immediately hinted very gently that port was not his drink, but his remark was either missed or good-naturedly overruled. 'Port is a man's drink.' I remember either Murry or Donald announcing in solemn tones. So port it was. And Lawrence drank it with the rest of us.

It had the effect of loosening at least some of the mute tongues about the table, though none of us women was perceptibly elevated. Lawrence began to talk in Spanish (which he had learned in Mexico). Donald, who prided himself on knowing a bit of Spanish (enough to read *Don Quixote* and to reply to simple questions) endeavoured to engage in Spanish conversation with Lawrence. This, for some reason, infuriated Kot to such a degree that he looked like taking the unwary Donald's life had not Murry tactfully placed somebody between them. Kot's idea seemed to be that the Spanish language was Lawrence's special perquisite. Gertler drank, or refrained from drinking, in silence, looking on, always looking on from a cold afar. Both he and Mary Cannan left early.

But not before this strange incident. It began with a speech by Kot in praise and love of Lawrence, the speech being punctuated by his deliberate smashing of a wine-glass at the close of each period. As—'Lawrence is a great man.' (Bang! down came Kot's strong fist enclosing the stem of a glass, so that its bottom came in shivering contact with the table.) 'Nobody here realises how great he is.' (Crash! another good wine-glass gone.) 'Especially no woman here or anywhere can possibly realise the greatness of Lawrence.' (Smash and tinkle!) 'Frieda does not count. Frieda is different. I understand and don't include her. But no other woman here or anywhere can understand anything about Lawrence or what kind of being he is.'

We women were silent. We felt, I think, very sympathetic to Kot. Anyhow I did. Sympathetic to his jealous, dark and overpowering affection—even inclined to agree with what he said.

Lawrence looked pale and frightfully ill, but his eyes were starry to an extraordinary degree. It occurred to me then—and I have since had no reason to change my reading, which was revealed as by the appearance of clear writing on the wall—that the deep hold of the Last Supper on the imagination of the world is not unconnected with the mystery of Bacchus. Given a man of genius; more especially given a man whose genius runs to expression by means of symbol, his essential utterance may well be achieved only when his genius is acted upon at a crisis by the magic of the fermented grape.

Anyhow, Lawrence who, like the others present, was habitually temperate, revealed that night at the Café Royal his deepest desire to all of us simply and unforgettably. And in doing so he brought about some other revelations, as will be seen.

Without making anything approaching a speech, he caught our attention by the quiet urgency of his request. What he said, in effect, was that we were his friends here, each and all of us people he had been very fond of. He could not stay in England. He must go back to New Mexico. Would we, would any of us, go with him? He asked each of us in turn. Would we go with him? Implicit in this question was the other. Did the search, the adventure, the pilgrimage for which he stood, mean enough to us for us to give up our own way of life and our own separate struggle with the world? Though his way of life must involve also a struggle with the world, this was not—as we well knew, its main objective. Rather was it a withdrawal of one's essential being from that struggle, and a turning of what strength one had into a new channel.

Essentially the appeal was not a personal one. Though it was to his friends, it was not for his sake or the sake of friendship that he made it. It was because of something in himself which we all acknowledged. But it had never before become so near being a personal appeal. It certainly had a personal element that told of his overwhelming loneliness. It was far less 'follow me' than 'come with me'. It was even—to my thinking at least— 'come for a time, and support me by your presence, as the undertaking is too much for me alone, yet I must not stay here with you'. I give my own reading, but I think something very like it was in the minds of all the others.

Remember we had just supped, and our glasses had been replenished with port, and, as I have said, we were all normally very abstemious people.

Mary Cannan was the only one to return a flat negative to Lawrence's question. It was as plump and plain as she herself was slender and pretty. 'No,' said she hardily. 'I like you, Lawrence, but not so much as all that, and I think you are asking what no human being has a right to ask of another.'

Lawrence accepted this without cavil or offence. It was a clear, hard, honest answer.

What Gertler said, I can't remember. I rather think it was a humouring but dry affirmative, which we all understood to mean nothing. Kot and Donald both said they would go, less drily, but so that any listener guessed they were speaking from goodwill rather than from deep intention. Dorothy Brett said quietly that she would go, and I, knowing that she would, envied her. Murry promised emotionally that he would, and one felt that he wouldn't. I said yes, I would go. And I meant it, though I didn't see how on earth it could be, anyhow for a long time. Unlike Mary and Dorothy Brett I had neither money of my own nor freedom from responsibility. Dorothy Brett, who loved to serve, was always coming to a loose end. I, who did not particularly like serving, was always having fresh responsibilities put upon me by life. Mary, disappointed with her 'freedom', had yet got used to its little self-indulgences and could not give them up. All the same I felt that Lawrence had somehow the right to ask me to go. And I feel to-day equally the impossibility of my going and the wish that I had gone.

As for the supper, what I next remember is Murry going up to Lawrence and kissing him with a kind of effusiveness which afflicted me. He must have been sensible to my feeling, because he turned to me.

'Women can't understand this,' he said. 'This is an affair between men. Women can have no part or place in it.'

'Maybe,' said I. 'But anyhow it wasn't a woman who betrayed Jesus with a kiss.'

At this Murry again embraced Lawrence, who sat perfectly still and unresponsive, with a dead-white face in which the eyes alone were alive.

'I *have* betrayed you, old chap, I confess it,' continued Murry. 'In the past I *have* betrayed you. But never again. I call you all to witness, never again.'

Throughout all this Frieda remained aloof and scornful—excluded. Her innings would be later. She reminded me of King David's wife looking down in derision from an upper window. One could not but admire her.

It must have been almost immediately after the strange episode with Murry, that Lawrence, without uttering a sound, fell forward with his head on the table, was deadly sick, and became at once unconscious. The combination of the port (which, when he had said he could not abide, he said truly) and the cruel loneliness which was brought home to him by the responses he had elicited from us, his friends, was too much for him.

In his sickness Lawrence was more like a child than a man. There was nothing disgusting about him. Frieda however, remained stonily detached, while Dorothy Brett and I ministered to him as best we could— she especially, who did not want me to help.

It must have been now that Mary and Gertler left us. What with the glasses broken by Kot, and Lawrence's sickness, I was sorry for the waiters who would have to clear up. But they behaved as if they had noticed nothing out of the way. Donald, as the soberest man, was handed money to pay for the wine and the damage. The bill, he tells me, struck him as wonderfully moderate.

We left in two taxi-cabs, Lawrence being still unconscious so that it was difficult getting him down in the lift. But Kot, even in liquor, was powerful. I recall that his legs seemed to fill the cab in which I was. I had been given all the hats of the party to hold, and I lost my own—a little real Russian cap of black astrakhan, which I liked better than any head covering I ever had, though I gave only three shillings for it in an antique shop, and it had a bullet-hole through it.

Arrived at Hampstead the problem was how to get Lawrence up to the first floor. Kot and Murry had to carry him. But in their enthusiasm they went on with their burden, up and up, till my brother, asleep on the top story, was awakened by the trampling, stumbling sound, and ran out in alarm to the little landing. He told me afterwards that when he saw clearly before him St John and St Peter (or maybe St Thomas) bearing between them the limp figure of their Master, he could hardly believe he was not dreaming. However, he conducted the party downstairs again.

Next morning soon after breakfast—certainly not later than 9.30 a.m.—I was passing the open door of the Lawrences' sitting-room, when Lawrence hailed me and bade me enter. He was fresh and serene. 'Well, Catherine,' he said, 'I made a fool of myself last night. We must all of us fall at times. It does no harm so long as we first admit and then forget it.'

At such times he was an overwhelmingly attractive human being. That light and easy, yet not flippant manner of his for dealing with such an incident, bespoke an underlying steadiness that begot trust in the on-looker and was—it seems to me—incompatible with any neurotic condition. Although the fullness of his admissions, and the sensitiveness of his abandon to the impulses of life might give to the superficial observer the impression that he was a sufferer from a neurosis, Lawrence was emphatically no neurotic. Of this I am convinced. If I add that he hated neurotics, even while he had the misfortune to find in them more immediately than in others a kind of response which sprang from superficial understanding, I suppose I shall call forth the gibe of the analyst—'Thou sayest it!' 'The real neurotic is half a devil,' said Lawrence, 'the cured one' with his 'perfect automatic control,' is 'a perfect devil.' And again, 'Spit on every neurotic and wipe your feet on his face if he tries to drag you down.' Yet I know that what I say is true. Lawrence hated, he feared, he fought and he was obliged to consort with neurotics. But he was himself untainted.

When I told him that I had lost my astrakhan cap he insisted on giving me two pounds to buy myself a hat. Unfortunately he did not like the one I bought, though he was too kind to say so. He liked a hat to be a hat, and to have a proper brim. This small black felt was brimless. He gave it a single glance and looked away. 'Quite saucy!' he said. I felt crushed.

NOTES

For a note on Catherine Carswell see p. 97. Lawrence arrived in England late in 1923 and within a few days (7 Dec 1923) wrote to Witter Bynner describing himself as 'perfectly miserable' (*Letters*, p. 589). Soon he was seeking kindred spirits who were prepared to drop everything and accompany him to New Mexico to found the colony of Rananim (see pp. 122–3). At this time the famous and bizarre Café Royal dinner, with its curious parallels to the Last Supper, took place. The account given by Catherine Carswell was bitterly disputed by J. M. Murry (*Reminiscences*, pp. 190–2), at least as far as his own part in the proceedings was concerned. He accused her of an 'abominable violation' and claimed that 'she suppressed Lawrence's words to me' (he had in mind the passage in which she quotes him as allegedly confessing to Lawrence that 'In the past I *have* betrayed you . . .'. He notes that he had previously written in *Son of Woman*, in a passage in which he appears to be 'speaking to Lawrence', 'Suddenly, you put your arm about my neck, for the first and last time, and said "Do not betray me!" ' He claims that the implication of Mrs Carswell's account is that he had 'deliberately falsified the happening'. He also quotes Lawrence, who wrote to him about a year later: 'You remember that charming dinner at the Café Royal that night? You remember saying: "I love you, Lorenzo, but I won't promise not to betray you"? Well, you can't betray me, and that's all there is to that . . . ' (*Letters*, pp. 636–7). Murry adds, 'These are the words I actually spoke'. On his efforts to suppress Catherine Carswell's book, see p. 97 above.

1. According to Moore (p. 322), Murry founded the *Adelphi*, which he edited from 1923 to 1930, 'to give Lawrence a voice'.

2. See p. 133.

3. See p. 112, n. 7.

4. The author had married Donald Carswell in 1915.

5. See p. 112, n. 4.

6. See p. 108, n. 2.

7. See p. 201.

8. The Oxfordshire home of Lady Ottoline Morrell (see p. 108).

9. The reference is to the poem 'On the Late Captain Grose's Peregrinations thro' Scotland'.

10. See p. 64, n. 9.

11. See p. 117.

12. Pseudonym of Pearl Craigie, a novelist who flourished in the 1890s.

The Café Royal Episode: Another Version*

DOROTHY BRETT

Murry is living in the house next door to me. He has a small room at the top of Boris Anrep's[1] house but he has his meals with me. Katherine's[2] rooms

* From *Lawrence and Brett: a Friendship* (London: Martin Secker, 1933) pp. 20–2, 23–4, 30–1.

are just as she left them, but Murry can never bring himself to use them much. He and I start for the Café Royal. A private room has been engaged, an ornate, over-gilded, red-plushed room. Koteliansky, Gertler and Mrs Gilbert Cannan are grouped round the fire with Catherine Carswell and her husband, Don. Koteliansky happy, exuberant; Gertler cheeky and gay; Mrs Cannan small and still lovely in evening dress with a large black picture hat. We wait, wondering whether you have got lost. A waiter suddenly flings open the door, and you are there. You step into the room, pause, and look at us all.

Slim, neat, with your overcoat folded over your arm, you stand looking at us, proudly, like a God, the Lord of us all, the light streaming down on your dark, gold hair. I turn away, strangely moved, while the others cluster round, one taking your hat, the other your coat; until, stepping out from among them, you say:

'Where is Brett? I want to meet her.'

I turn round, you come quickly forward, saying: 'So this is Brett.'

I look up, realising with surprise the eyes are blue, not black, as I had thought. How quick and eager and alert you are. I am to sit on your left and Mrs Cannan on your right; next her, Koteliansky, Don Carswell, Gertler, Catherine Carswell, Frieda, and Murry.

I put my ear machine on the table beside you; you look at it and laugh, a bit quizzically, making a few ribald remarks about the impossibility of making love into such a box. I, shy, attentive, silent, while you begin in your delicate, sensitive way to woo me. To what remark of mine do you reply, elfishly, mischievously, 'Ah, no, Brett, I am not a man...I am MAN.' And again and again: 'Will you come to Taormina with me, Brett; will you come? Or shall it be New Mexico?...But will you come or would you be afraid?' And I, overwhelmed, terribly aware of you, evading, dodging, murmur: 'I will go anywhere with you.'

'Would you be afraid to come to Taormina with me?'

'No. I would not be afraid,' comes my shy, nervous answer.

So around the table and around us goes the drink and laughter and talk. You make a speech, inviting all of us to go with you, to make a new life. Murry kisses you, fervently; Koteliansky makes a return speech; the glasses are flung over our shoulders, splintering on the floor.

Then, in the midst of it all, the wine gets the better of you, and you lean forward, dazed, and start vomiting, in the midst of a silent consternation. I take hold of your hand and hold it, with the other I stroke your hair, that heavy, dark, gold hair, brushing it back from your hot forehead. You are speechless, dazed, helpless, after you stop vomiting. Koteliansky and Murry carry you downstairs, into a taxi, and up the narrow stairs to your rooms at the top of Catherine Carswell's house in Hampstead. For several days you are sick in bed. I come to see you. You are sitting up in bed in a red knitted shawl, looking very pale and ill and hurt... You never spoke of it, nor we, and I never knew it happen to you again.

*   *   *

I am talking, in my sitting room, to a possible portrait client. The bell rings. I go to the front door and you are standing outside, looking with astonishment at the large Rolls Royce parked outside my door. May you come in? Of course. And in you come to find a lovely, though slightly faded woman sitting on my sofa. I introduce you to her by her married name, which means nothing to you as yours means nothing to her. She is talking about the portrait of myself, hanging above the sofa, and asks your opinion of it. Your laughing jeer fades away at my warning look, you bite your beard and say quickly: 'Oh, nice, quite nice; a very good likeness.' And she clinches the bargain with me, for which she has come—an order to paint her mother, to enable me to go to New Mexico.

You sit beside her on the sofa, and she, struck by your appearance—the beard, the rough hair, your midland accent—begins to question. 'Where do you come from?' Smiling you reply, 'The North Country, the Midlands.' She cannot make you out and you tell her that you write a bit. She is mystified and you are chuckling. After she leaves, I tell you that it is Edna May[3] the famous Belle of New York; and how delighted and amused you are at finding you had spent the afternoon with so famous an actress. And how disappointed that I had not told you at the time.

I have a kind of soirée one evening a week, Thursday, to which a chosen few come: Murry, Koteliansky, Gertler, and J. W. N. Sullivan[4] are the mainstay of it. A few other men add themselves to it later, and to these Thursdays no women are allowed, unless especially invited by the group. Frieda has not been invited; but when you came you are both invited and, after some hesitation, you both come. I think your curiosity brought you. We simply sit over the fire talking and drink tea—at least the men talk, and I try to listen in on my machine. To this gathering you come, and we sit around listening to your descriptions of New Mexico, the Mexicans and Indians. You get up and show us the curious tread of the Indian dance step, treading it slowly in a circle round the room, humming the Sun Dance song. Kot is angry, saying you belong to England, that you should live in England, that it is your right place; and you laugh, a tinge of bitterness in it, refusing to be held anywhere. Asking bitterly what has England ever done for you. Richard, Murry's young brother, says that if you would remain in England, he and many young men would follow you, that they need a leader. You jeer and reply that the young men do not want a leader; you know, only too well, what kind of a mess that leads to, and you wouldn't sacrifice your life for anything like that—oh, no, not for that. 'If the young men or anyone wants to follow me, let them. It's up to them. Let the dead bury their dead and the living follow me.'

*   *   *

Again we are sitting round your fire; it is cold. The chairs are few and we are many this evening. Murry, Koteliansky and Gertler seem to have absorbed all the chairs. You are sitting close to the fire pouring out the tea. The tea things are all on the grate. I sit on a stool next you. The room is cosy, darkly shadowed from the lamp on the table. Frieda is knitting. You are talking and laughing. I am trying to listen in with my machine. Gertler is impudent and gay; Koteliansky full of the fun of old days; Murry white and tired. The tea is so pale that you pour it back into the pot to let it stew. What are you talking about? I can't hear well enough. You seem to be talking for the moment on some favourite topic of yours, judging from the faces around. Suddenly Frieda begins attacking you, contradicting you, then denouncing you; finally accusing you of wanting to make a God of yourself, of being God. You expostulate wearily, you argue. From argument it turns to battle. Your temper rises to meet the sledge-hammer blows from Frieda's violent tongue. You break into the midland vernacular. The rich Yorkshire[5] dialect pours softly from your lips with an ever-increasing force, a steadily rising anger. In that language, strange to our ears, you fiercely denounce her. We sit and listen, spell-bound, until you suddenly seize the poker, and in a white heat of rage, you emphasise your words by breaking the cups and saucers. It becomes terrible to watch and to hear—the slow, deadly words and the steady smash of the poker, until, looking at Frieda, you say, slowly, menacingly:

'Beware, Frieda! If ever you talk to me like that again, it will not be the tea things I smash, but your head. Oh, yes, I'll kill you. So beware!' And down comes the poker on the teapot.

We are silent with consternation. No one speaks. You are silent, too, until, sighing heavily, you hold out your hand to me. I take it and silently hold it. Running your other hand through your hair, you give a little nervous laugh and say, 'Frieda should not make me so angry', and the evening almost regains its composure.

Later, Frieda, on her hands and knees, sweeps up the broken china with a dustpan and brush. But in all of us something seems to have been violated by our incapacity to protect you, by having to witness in silence the battle for your own existence. One by one the others get up and leave. Murry and I put on our coats. You come down the stairs with us; we go out into the deserted street.

'Strange, isn't it,' I say to Murry, 'to hear Lawrence use the 'thee' and 'tha' of the Yorkshire dialect?' Our departing footsteps echo on the frosty air. I turn and look back. You are standing on the steps in the bright moonlight . . . standing straight and arrowy before the shadowed doorway . . . faunlike.

NOTES

The Honourable Dorothy Brett (often known as 'Brett'), daughter of Viscount Esher, was educated at the Slade School and became a painter. She met Lawrence briefly in 1915 and renewed the acquaintance in 1923. In 1924 she went with the

Lawrences to New Mexico (having been the only one present at the Café Royal dinner to accept his invitation to follow them); she lived near them when they were at Kiowa Ranch and accompanied them to Mexico City, though in the face of Frieda's hostility she cut the trip short and returned to Taos. She was with the Lawrences again in Italy in 1926. She suffered from acute deafness.

    1. Mosaic artist of Russian origins.

    2. Murry's wife had died in 1923.

    3. Actress and star of *The Belle of New York*. She died in 1917, which suggests that this anecdote is not placed in chronological order but belongs to the period *circa* 1915.

    4. Author and journalist, friend of John Middleton Murry and a contributor to the *Athenaeum* and the *Adelphi*.

    5. Error for 'Nottinghamshire'.

In Hampstead[*]

DORA CARRINGTON

. . . I saw on Saturday afternoon D. H. Lawrence and his fat German spouse Frieda and the great decaying mushroom Middleton Murry and an attendant toadstool called Dr Young[1] at Brett's[2] house in Hampstead. I went up there to say goodbye to Brett, but found to my dismay this dreadful assembly of Adelphites.[3] Lawrence was very rude to me, of course, and held forth to the assembly as if he was a lecturer to minor university students. Apparently he came back this winter expecting to be greeted as the new messiah. Unfortunately very few saw his divination. The great Dunning[4] almost denied it. A few critics called him a genius but that wasn't enough. 'England is rotten, its inhabitants corrupt.' Mexico is the only country where prophets, and great writers are appreciated. So tomorrow Lawrence, and Frieda and Brett set off in an ocean liner for Mexico.

Of course on examination it comes out it is New Mexico that they go to, which is a state of USA. But they speak about it as 'Mexico'. 'We lead a very primitive life, we cut our own wood, and cook our own food' 'and Lawrence makes the mo-ost beau-ti-ful bread'. Frieda always comes in like a Greek chorus, the moment DHL has stopped speaking. I nearly said he could come to Tidmarsh[5] if that was all he wanted by 'Primitive'.

'And here is Carrington, not very much changed, lost a little of her

* From *Carrington: Letters and Extracts from Her Diaries*, ed. David Garnett (London: Jonathan Cape, 1970) pp. 283–4.

"ingenue" perhaps, still going to parties, still exactly the same, except I hear you are very rich now, and live in a grand country house.'

I took the shine off his Northampton[6] noise and his whining 'ingenue' accent. I told him I had £130 a year which I had always had. 'Ah but yer married a rich husband!' — 'He has £80 a year.'

'And yer don't mind the change, that's very fortunate.' I report this conversation so you can have an idea of the greatness of our present day geniuses.

He then gave a description of Mexico, with some fine literary passages at which all the assembly looked up and took notes in invisible note books. My brother Noel was at this strange tea party and of course was delighted at talking to the great D. H. Lawrence. Whenever DHL talked about the Mexican Indians, Noel made some absolutely boring remark about Hindus. If DHL described the Rockies and vegetation of the desert in Mexico, Noel at once described the Himalayas!!

The decayed Murry sat on a sofa and said nothing; he swayed backwards and forwards like a mandarin, with hollow eyes, toothless gums, a vacant smile and watery eyes. Only once he spoke. 'Say, Brett your butter's bad. It's not good.' (DHL. 'They've scalded it Brett, butter should'na be scalded. They've boiled the milk.') Otherwise the great Murry never spoke. It is reported he has given up the Adelphi and is, in a few months, going to follow the Messiah, Frau Messiah, and Brett to Mexico.

NOTES

Dora de Houghton Carrington, English painter born in 1893, preferred to be known by her surname. She was educated at the Slade School and became a close friend of Lytton Strachey—see Michael Holroyd, *Lytton Strachey: A Critical Biography*, II (London: Heinemann, 1968) *passim*. She committed suicide in 1932. The extract given above is taken from a letter to Gerald Brenan dated 4 March 1924; the meeting with Lawrence had taken place on 1 March. Dorothy Brett was also present and has given a brief account of the same tea-party (*Lawrence and Brett*, p. 28). It concludes, 'Carrington takes you [Lawrence] aside and begins archly to ask you about flowers. You are looking at her keenly. And I think you used her later in your story, "None of That".' In the story referred to (in the volume *The Woman who Rode Away*) Carrington appears as Ethel Cane; Aldous Huxley had also depicted her as Mary Bracegirdle in *Crome Yellow* (1921).

1. Dr J. C. Young had attended Katherine Mansfield during her last illness.
2. See p. 201.
3. The reference is to Murry's editorship of the *Adelphi* (see p. 133).
4. Unidentified.
5. Carrington lived at the Mill House in this Berkshire village.
6. Error for Nottingham.

'An Urge for Life'*

HARRIET MONROE

That March day in Chicago in 1924 was my only chance to verify by talk and the touch of eyes and hands the impressions gained through a desultory correspondence of ten years. I found a man uncannily active in spite of slight figure and frail health; with a loving observant eye, prehensile hands, a body alert and ready to leap like a cat, and a mind as taut as a steel spring. One felt an urge for life in his company; there was nothing sedative or soothing about this faun-like creature who wore no conventional veils over a spirit that darted this way and that to its discoveries. Nothing reminded one of his physical weakness; on the contrary he seemed lithe and extra-fit for dart and recoil—one had to sharpen one's paces to keep up with him. He looked like his pictures—the small face, triangular with its thick reddish hair and pointed beard, the narrow-chested thin-flanked body, the legs that seemed to clear the ground even when they rested. The contrast between his litheness and the solid well-rounded stability of his guardian wife was a lesson in the mystery of affinities.

* From an obituary of Lawrence published in *Poetry*, xxxvi (May 1930) pp. 93–4.

NOTE

Harriet Monroe, American poet and critic, founded and edited the magazine *Poetry*, to which Lawrence contributed. Her meeting with Lawrence in Chicago was on 19 March 1924; he had arrived in New York on 11 March and was proceeding to Taos.

In New Mexico Again*

DOROTHY BRETT

On May fifth [1924] we start for the Ranch.¹ Dates seem important to you: we had started from England on March the fifth, and you are struck by the coincidence.

What a start it is. In the early morning, the wagon with our trunks and stores drives off, driven by two Indians. The saddle-horses follow, as Mabel is lending us three of her horses: Bessie, Cequa and Poppy. Trinidad, wrapped in a gay blanket, rides one and leads the others.

We (and Mabel, with Tony driving) start later in the car. We overtake the wagon on the road. How gay the men look in their brilliant blankets. You are gay, too, excited, as change and movement always excite you. We are cumbered with packages and stores.

On reaching the Ranch, we begin at once to scrub out the solid hut. What a job it is. We work fearfully hard until twelve o'clock when the wagon arrives and we all have lunch.

*   *   *

'Brett, which of the cabins will you have?' you ask me as we stand looking at the little houses after our hard day's scrubbing and arranging. 'You can have either of these two. Frieda and I must have the large one, as we need a room each and a kitchen; but you can have either this one or the little one.'

I look around. Your long, straight cabin lies in the sunshine, the big, solitary pine in front of it, the shadow hardly falling on the house at all. Behind it are a few small pines. The big window of the sitting-room looks out across the field south to the Sangre de Cristo mountains. At the west end lies your bedroom, built of adobe; a big window on the west wall, another smaller one to the north, the door facing south. The kitchen at the east end of the house has but one window facing south alongside the door. Both the kitchen and the sitting-room are really one long log cabin, but now mere sheds.

To one side, but facing the big house, is the house you are now in: half adobe, the kitchen of wood. It lies deeply shaded under small fir trees, dark

---

* From *Lawrence and Brett*, pp. 67–72, 79–80, 82, 116–17, 134–8, 141–2, 229–30, 246–8.

and gloomy. The one room is biggish, the kitchen very small. Outside the white picket fence is the tiny tumble-down adobe house with a high-pitched shingle roof. There is something warm and sunny about it, the eastern window almost on the ground, level with the hillside, the south window and door just fitting into the length of it.

'I think I will have the little one,' I say. 'It's quite big enough, really, and I like the sunlight. This one under the trees is too gloomy.'

'All right,' you say, 'I will have a new roof put on it, and with a stove you ought to be all right. But some day we will have to clean the corral, that goat-dirt is too much. Five hundred goats—just think of it—and nothing been done for eight years, they say.' You add, doubtfully, that 'it is a healthy smell'.

The house question is settled, and we go to bed.

*   *   *

Thus the life at the Ranch begins. We work and toil, cleaning out the tumble-down cabins. The big one, full of cow-dung, is dilapidated, the lower logs of the long, back wall so rotten that they have to be taken out. Props are put in to hold up the walls as the rotten logs are carefully pulled out.

I am camping in the end room of the house, which is to be your bedroom: it is in fairly good condition. You and Frieda are in the other house, under the little pine trees. Mabel decides finally to camp with the Indians in Tony's big teepee up behind the cabins on the hill.

You spend most of your time working with the Indians. Trees have to be cut and stripped. It is all hard work, yet exciting. I gather stones for the new foundations. A trench is dug to keep the earth away from the new logs.

In the evenings we go up to the Indian Camp for supper. The Indians have built a half-circular screen of pine branches under a big pine tree. Inside they have laid skins and blankets. In front, a hole has been dug for the fire. A little further down the hill is the big Teepee and another half-circle of pine branches: in this, supper is cooking on a big fire. Frying pans with large steaks are sizzling. And we, very tired, are sitting around with our plates in our laps, waiting.

After supper we walk up the hill to the other camp and lie down on the blankets and skins. It is one of those magical evenings; a clear sky, a very young moon rising pale and slim out of the setting sun, a large star hanging below the moon. No sound, not a twig moves. The Indians are sitting in a row on a log, facing the setting sun. One of them rises and throws a great log on the fire, the flames leap high. The Indians are softly beating a small hand-drum, like a tambourine, and singing in their strange, haunting voices to the sinking sun. As the light fades, we all slip into shadow. The firelight catches your red beard and white face, bringing it suddenly out of the darkness. You are brooding, withdrawn, remote. Remote as the group of dark Indians are remote in their ecstasy of singing, the firelight playing on their vivid blankets, the whites of their eyes. I am caught and held by your brooding face. All of us are caught and held by the rhythm, the Indian rhythm, as if the very earth itself were singing.

*   *   *

The days are long and hot. The cabin is built up slowly. I chop wood for Frieda's little kitchen stove. You are working all day with the Indians. Frieda cooks, lies on her bed smoking, cooks again.

One of the worst jobs of all is cleaning out the roof of the big house. It is like an oven between the roof and the tin ceiling. With a handkerchief bound round your mouth, you have been sweeping the rat-dirt and nests out with a small dust-pan and brush. You come crawling out, looking white and tired. Candido remonstrates with you and says he will go in. I fetch another handkerchief which you tie round his face, over his mouth. In he goes. You climb onto the tool-shed roof and peer through the little door at him. He comes out a bit later, sweat pouring down his face, gasping, a pile of nests in the dust-pan.

Nothing will prevent you from doing the same hard work that the Indians do, however dirty and disagreeable. You have to share the worst with the best, even the dirt and heat in the roof. You will not ask the Indians to do anything that you are not willing to do yourself. And you insist on giving them plenty to eat.'They must have something to grind their bellies on,' you tell Frieda.

You have bad headaches, and bad neuralgia, yet you work persistently. The Indians work willingly and happily with you and they like you; and until you are told that they laugh at you behind your back, you like them enormously. But that hurts you—always you are sensitive to being laughed at.

Gradually, out of the chaos, the cabin begins to shape. I suggest a fireplace in the back wall before the logs are placed. Full of excitement, you hurry to the Indians. 'Is it possible?' you ask. They say it is quite easy and a huge fireplace is planned. Then I have another inspiration: a window in the back wall of the kitchen. That, too, is easy. The new logs are put in place, then the hole for the fireplace is sawed out and the hole for the window.

Into the fine hot days, great storms come crashing. On such evenings the Teepee leaks and Mabel goes down to Taos. She takes the list for stores. When she returns, she brings the stores with her, and sometimes more Indians. The tent dries out quickly, but the storms come up unexpectedly and sometimes so late that Mabel in her tent is taken unawares. Then she has a cot in your kitchen, although I offer her a place in my room.

*   *   *

There is, even with all the Indians, much work to be done. Wood for the stove has to be chopped small, water carried from the spring. I look after the wood and water. You are away most of the day in the woods, cutting down trees with the Indians. Frieda cooks and lies on her bed smoking her endless cigarettes. Mabel and Tony go to and fro to Taos in their car, taking Indians away, bringing them back with more stores, more pots and pans and comforts.

When Mabel is away, we have supper in the little kitchen; the Indians carry theirs to their camp. This evening I lay the table in the kitchen. Mabel and Tony are in Taos. I sharpen the knives; Frieda is fussing round the stove; you are washing outside in a small basin, kneeling on the ground.

When supper is ready, we sit down, tired—oh, so tired—and eat, too tired to talk. Afterwards, as we wash up, you begin to sing. The dishes finished, we sit down and sing. We sing old Scotch songs, old English songs and ballads. Suddenly there is a knock on the door and Candido and the other Indians ask to come in. They have heard the singing and feel lonely. Candido has a badly swollen finger, poisoned. You look at it carefully and tell him it is dangerous, that you must poultice it. Frieda puts some milk on to boil; then some bread is soaked in it; and you cut up a clean linen handkerchief. Gently, and with deft, careful fingers, you wash the wound and lay the boiling poultice on the finger. Candido draws back with a cry; you blow on the poultice, lifting it off his finger. Taking hold of his hand, you tell him to warn you when it gets too hot. Slowly you lower it again until it rests lightly on the finger. Candido screws up his face, but says nothing. You press the poultice slowly onto the finger and hold it there. During the evening you renew the poultice three times, finally bandaging the hand up in the last one.

'Don't take it off,' you say to Candido, 'I will make you a new one tomorrow.'

* * *

We are sitting in the lamplight round the table. You are talking of Italy and somehow of St Francis of Assisi.

'Think,' you say, 'how horrible, kissing the leper; kissing that filthy disease with one's sensitive lips.' You shudder. 'And then eating dirt—dirt, with the sensitive membrane of one's mouth. It's just disgusting, loathsome; and makes me sick in my stomach.' Frieda and I are silent: it certainly is sickening.

'*Ulysses*,'[2] Frieda shouts, suddenly. 'Have you read *Ulysses*, Brett? It is a wonderful book.' You look at me, steadily, a quiet, penetrating look. Before I have time to answer Frieda, you say vehemently:

'The last part of it is the dirtiest, most indecent, obscene thing ever written. Yes it is, Frieda,' you continue, sharply. 'It is filthy.'

A tremendous power pours out of you. I stick my nose back into my book. Something warns me to say nothing as to whether I have read the book or not. You read on slowly through a story in the magazine *Adventure*. At your elbow lie some books that Mabel has sent up.

'*The Golden Bough*,'[3] you say suddenly, 'How I hate these people who write books from their armchairs; men who never go out and experience anything for themselves. They just sit at home and write about everything second-hand, never having seen an Indian or a tiger or known anything. What's the good of that? They are afraid to meet life, to experience it for themselves.' Frieda stitches away silently. I look up and say:

'Didn't Fenimore Cooper[4] know Indians?'

'No, never,' you say abruptly. 'I doubt if he ever saw one. Haven't you read my Essays?'[5] And you return angrily to your magazine and read slowly, slowly. I marvel always at the slowness of your reading.

[After supper we] sit for awhile in the dim light of the oil lamp and talk. 'I know, Brett,' you say crisply. 'I know you believe in friendship. I don't— oh, no, not for me. I don't want love; I don't want anybody's love or friendship; I just don't believe in it.'

'It *is* possible,' I say, weakly, 'I am sure it is.'

'Perhaps for you, but not for me. Oh, no, not for me.'

What is wrong with people and friendship has been the argument of the moment.

'If people were like horses or cats or any wild animal,' you continue. 'If they were as natural. A horse is never anything but itself; it is true to form always. It never swerves from its pattern, its horsiness. That is the difference. Human beings are always untrue to their pattern; they have ceased to have a pattern. A man is no longer MAN. A tiger in the jungle is always a tiger, but men you can't trust—they always let you down and themselves.'

I make no answer. I think of the trust you have, the way you always go out to people, hopefully and eternally.

'You are too romantic, Brett,' you add, after a while. 'You are always so romantic,' you continue, a bit scornfully.

'So are you,' I retort. 'I am no more romantic than you are.'

'Oh, yes you are,' you reply, sardonically; but you give me a mischievous, sly side-glance. I laugh and you laugh. Both of us know that neither of us will admit that we are romantic.

* * *

To-day you are going to bake. This morning you mixed the flour and put the basin in the sun for the bread to rise. By the afternoon it is all swelled up and ready, so I run around for wood and you light the fire. The flames are huge in the oven and your eyes are watering from the smoke that pours out of the little hole at the side and of course blows your way. It is rather wonderful and mysterious: the flames are beautiful in the dark oven, with occasional splashes of sunlight on them. And you, with your smudged face, long forked stick, and sandalled feet, poking at the sticks in the oven, are more Pan-like than ever.

After about an hour of this, you let the fire die down and rake out the hot ashes. In goes one of our precious chickens and the bread. The board that serves as a door is quickly closed, and the large stone put against it. Then you sit down and wait. While waiting, you tell me how when quite tiny, only just able to see over the edge of the table, you would watch your mother making the bread. I run for my kodak and take a photo of you sitting on the shed step, near the oven.

Frieda is cooking the vegetables, so I go in and lay the table and sharpen the knives. In about half an hour, you take out the chicken and the bread. The chicken is tender and done to a turn; the bread is perfect. You are immensely proud of yourself. Our chicken and meat days make us feel. fine—they come so seldom!

* * *

You suddenly spit. You constantly spit, so there is nothing new in that: but this time a splash of bright red blood comes with it, which is new. You cast a look of consternation at Frieda: she looks flabbergasted—while I pretend not to see at all. You already have a bit of a cold, and during the morning this gets worse. After lunch, looking white and ill, you go to bed and there you stay, sleeping most of the day.

The following day you are still in bed, and in the afternoon you spit blood again. When Spud[6] and I ride for the milk, Frieda sends a message to Bill [Hawk] to ask him if he will drive in to the Hondo and telephone for the Doctor. When we get back, you are sitting up in bed with your supper tray on your lap. Frieda calls to us to ask if the Doctor can come. With a violence that is overpowering, you break in, turning on Frieda in a wild fury:

'What do you *mean*? Why have you sent for the Doctor?' You are sitting up straight, tense with rage; your voice shrills out: 'How *dare* you!' And you pick up the iron egg ring that serves you for an egg-cup, and hurl it at Frieda's head. It misses her by the fraction of an inch and almost falls into Spud's open mouth as he stands aghast and astonished that weak and ill as you are, you have the strength to be so furious.

'You *know* I dislike Doctors. You *know* I wouldn't have him or you wouldn't have sent for him behind my back. I *won't* see him—I *won't*!' Your voice is shrill, the sentences seem to explode from you. 'I'll go out and hide in the sage brush until he goes. I'll teach you!'

Spud and I look at each other, helplessly. Frieda is murmuring in a flustered, bewildered way.

'But Lorenzo, I was worried about you. It won't do any harm. If it's nothing, we'll all be relieved; and if it's serious, the doctor can help.'

A dead silence. Frieda comes hurrying out of your room, her eyes darting in all directions. You, quiet now, lie looking out through the open door, sore, angry and helpless. Only partially resigned to your weakness and helplessness.

Frieda, Spud and I, dismayed and worried, have supper; then wait for the doctor. It grows dark and I stand behind the big tree, watching the headlights of a car coming across the desert. I peep occasionally round the tree trunk to look into your lighted room. You are sitting up in bed, wrapped in a shawl, looking hurt and miserable.

The lights on the desert disappear, to reappear in three quarters of an hour through the trees across the field. The trees light up, and the glaring headlights of the car blaze onto the field. It is Dr Martin driven by Clarence. They have blankets in the car, as Dr Martin fears pneumonia; and in that case wants to take you down to Taos where Mabel is warming more blankets.

Old Martin marches into your room and the door shuts. Behind the tree I wait, until the door opens again and the light streams out. I peep round, cautiously. You are sitting up in bed, the tension gone; the grimness has left your face and you are smiling. A sort of ease and repose has spread over you. I can feel it from where I am: it spreads into the night, as the light from your door spreads into the darkness. Old Martin comes out, smiling too; and Clarence drives him away.

*   *   *

I go in to Frieda. She is beaming.

'It is all right,' she tells me. 'Nothing wrong; the lungs are strong. It is just a touch of bronchial trouble—the tubes are sore. I am making him a mustard plaster and you must ride down tomorrow to Rachel and borrow some mustard from her, as I have no more.' Lord, what a relief!

Down I go next morning for the mustard. And in the afternoon, Spud and I pick masses of raspberries up in the canyon behind the houses, while you are still in bed with a large mustard plaster biting your chest.

*   *   *

You begin to mend; but I am still cautious about going in to talk to you. I can never forget Katherine Mansfield breaking a blood-vessel talking to me. But I find a little humming bird fluttering on my window in my house. I catch it and am amazed at its lightness; holding it carefully, I hurry over to your house and take it to you.

'What is it?' you ask.

'Be careful,' I reply, 'and don't let it fly away. Hold out your hands.' I place the bird carefully in them, and you sit there holding it. A look of amazement, followed by another of almost religious ecstasy comes into your face as the tiny fluff of feathers sits in your hand, the long beak tapering and sharp, the gorgeous metal splendour of the green and blue throat shimmering.

Suddenly, with a laugh, you toss it into the air. The bird, its invisible wings humming, hums its way through the door away into the air with its long, looping flight.

*   *   *

We are having a cold lunch of hard-boiled eggs and cold meat on the porch, waiting for Mabel to come and take you and Frieda to the Hopi Snake Dance. She is bringing two Indian women to stay with me, as I am not included in the party to the dance. It means a trip of nearly two weeks across the desert. You are taking camping things, blankets and food and water. There is no water in the desert on the way to the pueblos you are going to. It is a long, hot drive, over rough roads, through arroyos, sometimes through quicksand. Rough, hot, and tiring, but well worth while—so Mabel tells you—to see the Snake Dance of the Hopi Indians. As we eat, you tell me some of those rare tales of your childhood.

'As a baby of four,' you say, 'I would run away from my sisters, escaping whenever I could, and run down the road to the old, disused railway level-crossing. I would crouch down, peering through the bars of the gate, waiting for a train to come by, to watch the wheels against the sky. The line was on a high embankment—I could see the wheels and it was the fast-turning wheels against the sky that fascinated me; that and the deep rumble of the train. There I would sit until my sisters found me and carried me home.' Then you would add bitterly and angrily: 'You children brought up by nurses and in nurseries, what do you know of life? What do you know of the mechanics of life? Nothing—nothing! You take no part in the actual work of everyday living. I hate your class—I hate it!' Then you continue:

'As a boy, I would play hide-and-seek with the other boys after dark. On dark evenings, we would run among the hedges and trees, with the lights of the town in the distance. It was lovely, very lovely to be running in the rain or in the moonlight, with the faint calls of the other boys, and the lights of the town twinkling in the distance. Lovely, and a bit scaring, too. And perhaps, on the whole, the happiest time of my life.' You sigh heavily. 'Maybe the only time I have known real happiness. And it was real life, not a false life, like yours has been.'

*   *   *

What a party. You are all dressed up in a clean white shirt, blue velvet French trousers, cowboy boots and big Stetson. The trousers I have lent you. I bought them in 1915 in Paris, when I went with my father during the war.

Margaret Hale and Mrs Swain have come to fetch Friedel.[7] He is to stay with them a day or two before he starts back to Germany. Everybody is gay, but as Friedel clicks his heels and bows to each one of us in turn, Frieda's eyes fill with tears, for she is sad at his going. He leans out of the car, waving, until the trees swallow him up.

We go in and make some tea. You are in great spirits, hoping when you get to England to make every one of your old friends hate you. We laugh at the thought of making them wither and you are keen to knock them all off their perches. Then we start an argument about Christ. You get furious with me because I stick up for Christ, and maintain it was his disciples that made him so soft.

'No,' you say, angrily, 'Christ was a rotter, though a fine rotter. He never *experienced* life as the old Pagan Gods did. His merit was that he went through with his job: but that was soft, squashy, and also political—a Labour leader. He never knew animals, or women, from a child—never. He held forth in the Temple and never *lived*. Oh, basta! He was out to die, that's what makes his preaching disastrous.'

'But,' I begin.

'But what!' you chip in quickly. 'It's no good, Brett. I know.' And that was that: And now Frieda is waxing indignant at the way you are treated by your friends, insisting that you ought not to believe in them.

'No,' you say, emphatically. 'I must believe in people, even though in the end I may be cheated. I cannot go through life suspecting people.'

*   *   *

To-day you are both tired. Frieda is tidying the barn, you are chopping wood. I go into the kitchen. I look round, feeling something is missing. You have come in behind me and are watching me. Then I know. The green dish from Oaxaca is gone. A grim smile lights up your face.

'It fell off the table,' you say, whimsically; adding grimly, 'that made me so mad that I smashed it with the axe.' I look horrified; it was a lovely dish. 'People come,' you continue, 'and they suck the life out of me, to bring life into themselves. I am tired, sick to death of people and everything. I don't want to go to England. I wish I could go straight to Italy. America irritates me with her gold standard. I am tired, tired...' You get up and, picking up the axe, you go back to your chopping.

I look for Frieda in the barn. She smiles a bit nervously. She is sitting smoking on a trunk. I sit down on another.

'I am not used,' she says, 'to playing second fiddle. Always at home I played first fiddle. When I again saw my children after all those years, they said how surprised they were to see me playing second fiddle. I am as important as Lawrence, he says so himself. At school in Germany, all the children did as I told them; they believed in me. But I am just as important as Lawrence, don't you think so?'

'We all are,' I reply. 'In one way—in ourselves. But not, perhaps, in another. He is a great creative artist; that makes a difference.' Frieda ponders a while over this.

'He always wants to boss,' she says at last, then throws her cigarette away and dumps the contents of a trunk on to the floor. The tidying of the barn proceeds.

*　*　*

You are sad and depressed at the going of Dan. Now that I have Prince and you have Ambrose as well as Aaron, I have returned Dan to the Waynes. We none of us need him. You are really upset at his going as the Wayne girl leads him away across the field. You hurry off into the woods. The next time I meet you, you are carrying Smoky, the hen, headless and with wings still flapping.

'I chopped off her head,' you say, 'to relieve my feelings. She was getting broody, and then I hate them.' Frieda, for some unknown reason, flies into a temper and rants at you, shouting that you are a nuisance and always laying down the law. That wearies you and you pay no attention. I am tired with a headache.

We get our horses, you and I, and ride for the milk. You unsaddle Prince for me and leave me in my cabin in the orchard. Then, with a wave of the hand and a cheery good-night, you ride home and I go to bed.

NOTES

For a note on Dorothy Brett see p. 201.

1. Kiowa Ranch in the Sangre de Cristo Mountains, New Mexico. The Lawrences and Dorothy Brett arrived in Taos in March 1924; relations between 'Brett' and Mabel Luhan (see p. 171) soon became strained, so that it was a relief to the English party to leave for the ranch, which had been given by Mrs Luhan to Frieda.

2. Published in 1922. For Lawrence's adverse opinion of Joyce's later work, see *Letters*, pp. 742, 751.

3. This monumental anthropological work by J. G. Frazer appeared between 1890 and 1915.

4. American novelist (1789–1851), author of *The Last of the Mohicans* and other popular works.

5. Lawrence's *Studies in Classic American Literature* (1923) contains two essays on Fenimore Cooper.

6. See p. 191, n. 4.

7. Friedrich Jaffe, a nephew of Frieda, spent the summer of 1925 with the Lawrences at Kiowa Ranch.

An Interview with Lawrence*

KYLE S. CRICHTON

We waited patiently in the car until at last we saw a figure flying down the hill toward us. It was Lawrence, waving his arms jovially and showing by his actions that we were not only welcome but had possibly rescued them in the nick of time. He was at the car before we could scramble out and was in time to help my wife crawl down.

He was thin, about five eight in height, and had a dark reddish beard and the same wart on the right side of his face that appears in all his photographs. He was wearing a blue denim shirt, buttoned at the neck but without a tie, brown striped pants that obviously belonged to an old suit, black woollen socks and sandals. His lips were full and quite red; his eyes were small but astonishingly bright and blue, and he looked steadily at you when he talked. When we reached the little clearing by the house, Frieda, his wife, was there to greet us and was as friendly as Lawrence himself. She was a large handsome woman and spoke with a decided German accent.

I had no faintest idea how to begin an interview, but that was not necessary, for we sat in the porch which seemed built as an indentation of the cabin, and started talking naturally. We first spoke of Harvey Fergusson's *Women and Wives*[1] because he was a New Mexican author and Lawrence said somebody had sent him the book. He said he thought it was 'thin' and then, probably out of a feeling he was being harsh with a young author and possibly my friend, he added hastily that early reviewers of his novels used to refer to them contemptuously as 'Zolaesque'.

'Zolaesque!' I said in surprise, for it seemed the last thing anybody would say about a Lawrence novel.

'They thought it would put me down,' said Lawrence, 'but I took it as a compliment. I thought highly of Zola then, and I still do.'

From that he went on to telling how his first work saw print. He was engaged to a girl in the little town of Eastwood, while he was teaching school at Croydon and detesting it. Since he was twenty-three and in the proper mood, he conducted his courtship in rhyme. Without telling Lawrence what she had done, the young lady sent the poems to Ford Madox Hueffer, who immediately accepted them for his magazine and published them in the next issue. Hueffer then wrote Lawrence asking him

*From Nehls, ii, pp. 411–18.

to call. This was an important moment in Lawrence's life, for Hueffer was the first literary person he had met. He was astonished by Hueffer and now when he was telling us about the interview, he began mimicking Hueffer, screwing an imaginary monocle in his eye and talking in the humph-humph almost unintelligible way that Ford's friends remember so well.

'Hueffer lives in a constant haze,' said Lawrence. 'He has talent, all kinds of it, but has everlastingly been a damned fool about his life. He's fine in half a dozen lines of writing but won't stick to any one of them, and the critics can't stand that in a writer.'

'His wife's very nice,' Frieda said.

'Why the devil he ever married Violet Hunt!'[2] cried Lawrence, throwing up his hands. 'Why, she's too devilishly clever for a man ever to want to marry.'

Lawrence could see that we were not too well acquainted with Violet Hunt and added that she was a novelist and quite good—much better than May Sinclair, for instance.

'Why do you like Sinclair so much over here?' he wanted to know. 'It's a mystery. You should see her...a little humped up scrawny woman. Oh, married, of course, but she could never be anything but a spinster.'

He then launched into a long defence of Violet Hunt as a novelist, saying that she wasn't at all appreciated properly.

'Maybe it's because of Hueffer?' suggested Brett.

'Ah, perhaps,' conceded Lawrence. 'That Hueffer...a born romanticist. When Stepnyak, the Russian, was sounding Hueffer for information about English farming and happened to mention rye, Hueffer said, "Yaws, yaws...rye...rye is one of our-ah-lawgest crops..." And rye,' Lawrence shouted with merriment, 'there isn't half an acre of rye in all England. It just struck Hueffer that it would be a fine thing for England to have acres of rye and he couldn't help telling Stepnyak.'[3]

'Do you remember the time he came with Garnett[3] at the first of the war and Mrs Wells was there?' asked Frieda sourly. 'I mentioned something about Germany and he puffed up right away and started talking about his Dutch relatives. Before he had always kept German servants and blasted the British Empire and said he wasn't a subject of the King and spoke German at the table—and now he was Dutch. It was enough for me.'

Although he had been known as Ford Madox Ford for at least ten years, the Lawrences always referred to him as Hueffer. That might be part of Frieda's revenge or because they had always known him by the former name, but Lawrence said something then that showed he was still fond of Ford, with all his faults.

'A bit of a fool, yes,' he conceded, 'but he gave me the first push and he was a kind man.'

The reference to Garnett got Lawrence started again on reminiscences and he told how he had met Garnett through Hueffer and had been guided by him in his first years as a writer.

'Garnett did a great deal for me,' said Lawrence. 'He was a good friend and a fine editor, but he ate his heart out trying to be a writer. When I'd visit them, I'd find Garnett in his study, spending hours working over a single phrase to get the very last quality of rightness. He would rack his brain and suffer while his wife, Constance Garnett, was sitting out in the garden turning out reams of her marvellous translations from the Russian. She would finish a page, and throw if off on a pile on the floor without looking up, and start a new page. That pile would be this high...really, almost up to her knees, and all magical.'

In my guise as an interviewer, I managed a few stupid questions on his own method of writing and learned that he did everything by pen—a fat red full-barrelled fountain pen. When I asked if he dictated, there was amusement all around.

'It's a private joke of our own,' explained Lawrence. 'Frieda and I were once staying with Compton Mackenzie[4] and at two in the morning we came on Compton in bed in silk pajamas—eh, Frieda?—with Brett Young's brother, his secretary, taking notes and Mrs Mackenzie, two rooms away, playing softly and romantically on the piano. Ho! If I wrote like that something fantastic would come out!'

That prompted me to ask about Michael Arlen,[5] who was then the English literary sensation, and I was surprised to hear that they knew him quite well.

'The pride of Mayfair,' said Lawrence, 'and when we first knew him he hadn't even *seen* an aristocrat. He was a nice young fellow, who was making a literary living on odds and ends, but when we next saw him he came to our house in Poland[6] in riding togs. I'm sure he had never ridden a horse in his life, but there he was in riding breeches with loud black and white checks and a pointed hat with a feather—like an old time chevalier. His popularity comes from catering to the petty vice instinct in people, but his reputation is beginning to wane.'

And then he added something that shocked me.

'That's also true of Katherine Mansfield's reputation,' he said. 'She was a good writer they made out to be a genius. Katherine knew better herself, but her husband, John Middleton Murry, made capital of her death. Murry was a strange one,' he concluded.

They were still very pleased with a visit from Willa Cather[7] some weeks before. She had made the hard trip up the mountain and later had sent the book of her own she liked best—*The Song of the Lark*.

'We had been warned that we might not like her,' said Frieda. 'Everybody said she was blunt and abrupt, but we got along famously.'

That got us on to the mechanics of writing, which they said they had discussed with Miss Cather, and Lawrence said it was fine for him to have an agent like Curtis Brown,[8] for he was practically helpless as a business man. When a book was once sent away, he forgot about it.

'No, not entirely,' he amended. 'There are the proofs, which I don't mind so much when they're fresh and I'm still afire over the work. But it's awful to read stuff when it's once in book form. Last year in Mexico I reread *The White Peacock* for the first time in fifteen years. It seemed strange and far off and as if written by somebody else. I wondered how I could have thought of some of the things or how I could have written them. And then I'd come on something that showed I may have changed in style or form, but I haven't changed fundamentally. Reviews? No, I never read them any more and care almost nothing about what people say.'

That brought one of my bright moments, and I had the wit to ask what made a writer write. The meeting perked up immediately.

'Egotism,' said Frieda flatly.

'No, no,' protested Lawrence. 'It isn't that. You don't write for anybody; you rather write from a deep moral sense—for the race, as it were.'

'And to let everybody know how clever you are,' persisted Frieda.

Brett had left her spot behind the little table and now edged her way forward with her horn cocked for battle and a happy smile on her face.

'Of course, you want to see it published,' admitted Lawrence, 'but you don't really mind what people say about it. It doesn't *matter* what they say. A writer writes because he can't help writing, and because he has something in him that he feels he can say better than it has been said before, and because it would be wrong, entirely wrong, to possess a talent and have thoughts without sharing them with the world.'

'But how about the time you stopped for a year!' demanded Frieda. 'You were angry at what people said then.'

This was a reference to the banning of *The Rainbow* in England on moral grounds, a blow from which Lawrence had trouble in recovering. His face clouded and his tone changed.

'No, Frieda,' he said in a sad voice. 'Not angry. That was an entirely different thing. They were robbing me of my freedom then.'

'But you were bitter,' insisted Frieda, in a way that showed she was still steaming over the incident.

'No, not bitter, Frieda,' he said, and laughed. 'Bored—just bored.'

And he did strike you as a man who had arranged his life so that blows would have little effect on him. Since the scene had been a little tense, I sought to bring in a touch of small talk. I let drop the information that Sousa and his band were to appear in Albuquerque that winter.

'Sousa!' cried Lawrence, starting up. 'He must be a hundred. Sousa—himself? Is he still living?'

' "Stars and Stripes Forever" ' put in Brett happily.

And Frieda could remember the stir the band had made when it came to Germany—oh, years ago.

'The little hats and the smart uniforms and the little man with the beard going on ahead. It just doesn't seem possible. He *can't* be alive!'

I assured them he was and added that we would also be favoured by a visit from the Barnum and Bailey and Ringling Brothers circus. This was almost too much for them.

'Barnum and Bailey—ooh!' shouted Frieda and Brett simultaneously. A hubbub set up as they compared notes on how many times they had seen Barnum and Bailey and how wonderful it had been and how they wished they could see it again.

'For years that's all I knew about America,' said Brett. 'Barnum and Bailey and Sousa.'

'Oh, now, let's be fair,' said Lawrence laughing. 'There was James Fenimore Cooper.'

Frieda and Brett made motions of the face, as if to say that certainly they had read Cooper but Cooper after all wasn't what appealed to girls. Lawrence seemed to feel that he had put them at a disadvantage and added hastily:

'I like the trapeze fellows—those men who fly through the air and grasp their partners en route. A very high and wonderful art!'

How it followed from this conversation is not clear, but I took this chance of asking what they read in their mountain home. This is when I got my second serious shock.

'You'll never guess,' said Lawrence. 'Here!'

He thrust into my hand a copy of *Adventure* magazine, which at that time was edited by the late Arthur Sulivant Hoffman.

'Not bad, either,' said Lawrence. 'The writers are very lively and they are honest and they are accurate about their facts. If they say something happened in a certain way in Africa or Malaya, you can depend on it. If they're wrong, the readers pick them up mighty fast.'

What about the better known American magazines, I asked, trying not to show my horror and pain. Lawrence made a wry face.

' "With milk and honey blest," ' he said.

As for books, the Lawrences said they read whatever anybody sent them. At the moment they had only about ten books in the house.

'We never carry any when we travel,' said Lawrence, 'and take whatever our kind friends foist off on us. In that way we learn things we'd never in a hundred years pick off a library shelf.'

When we went into the house later, it was so immaculate, so scrubbed and shining, that we immediately attributed it in our minds to Frieda's German upbringing. It turned out to be Lawrence's doing almost entirely.

'You'd never think it of him,' said Frieda proudly, when Lawrence went out to get things ready for tea, 'but he's the most practical man I've ever known . He made the bread this morning in the Indian oven just outside the door there, milked Susan and looked after the chickens. I cook when he'll let me, but he does it much better himself. When you get a chance, look at the new cow shed and say a word about it. He's very proud of that; he did it all with his own hands.'

In the course of this, Brett had broken into a special sort of smile, a meaningful smile, and when we looked at her inquiringly, she said, 'Susan', and it was plain that the cow was a cross Lawrence had to bear. At that moment he came in from the kitchen and said in a voice of fake indignation: 'The bloody beast...Had to chase her two full hours this morning. If we tether her, she either breaks the rope or gets so tangled up we're afraid she'll choke herself.'

By now Lawrence was laying down the tea things and in a few minutes was cutting bread from a huge loaf in the thinnest daintiest slices. The bread was delicious, the raspberry preserve was wonderful and the tea was fine, if one liked tea.

'You can thank Brett for the berries,' said Frieda. 'Picked them on the hill here back of the house. Lorenzo did the preserving.'

'They'll think you do nothing in the place,' Lawrence reminded her.

'If they've ever lived on a farm, they won't,' said Frieda.

We said we had never lived on a farm and after hearing about Susan weren't sure the idea appealed to us.

'If it isn't Susan, it's the pack rats,' said Lawrence. 'Look up there.'

In the ceiling of the room was a series of large hooks, which we looked at with wonder and lack of understanding.

'When we leave here, said Lawrence, 'we lash everything up to those hooks like sides of beef in a shop...chairs, divan, tables. If we didn't we'd come back to find everything gone. They literally eat a chair right down to the last rung. Big monsters, as large as a dog.'

We refrained from saying that this was an additional reason for not living on a farm, but Frieda caught the look and laughed.

'They're not the kind that run up a skirt,' she said, 'and they stay away when we're here. But I suppose if they ever took it into their heads, they could run right over us.'

Since I come from a coal mining family, I had wanted from the beginning to discuss the subject with Lawrence, whose father was a miner, but had held back for fear he might have bad memories of the life. But he was interested immediately and began talking in an eager way.

'It's not the nicest life,' he said, looking at me as if he thought I might have other ideas, 'but the miner has a fuller life than the middle class or the aristocrat has. When they're down there in the earth, they're like little kings. They work alone and their wives aren't there to boss them and it's man against nature and man against fate. They have a full inner life, with their own thoughts and crotchets and independences, but they have this fullness only up to a certain point and then it quits. Then everything becomes narrow and restricted. We go back to see my sister who keeps a shop in a little coal town, but I'm never able to stay more than a day. It depresses me.'

He said his family could never get accustomed to his being a famous man and a writer. Anyone who has read *Sons and Lovers* will know how close Lawrence was to his mother, and he told us how sad he had been that she had died three days before his first book was published. She would have understood, but the others looked on him as sort of a freak.

'I took my father a book and he said, "What might you be getting for a wee bit book like that, David lad?" and I said, "Two hundred pounds, Father," and he said that convinced him that not all the fools were dead in the world.'

Lawrence acted out the Midland dialect and gave the last words in a tone of real disgust.

Frieda said they hadn't been in to Taos for a month and had no desire to go in. They had their horses and once a week they rode into the little town of Arroyo Hondo to buy their groceries. This brought on talk of prices in America as compared with England, and Lawrence said that for a two-year period they had lived in England on fifty pounds a year (then about $250).

'Both of you!' I exclaimed.

'Yes,' laughed Lawrence. 'It could be done. We did it.'

'Tell him about the man who wanted to guarantee us the rich life,' said Frieda ironically.

'Ah, yes; him,' said Lawrence grinning through his beard. 'He said it was the duty of a nation to protect its geniuses and said that we should have, say, two hundred and fifty pounds a year as a steady income. More, he added, would not be good for us.'

When we went out on the porch again the sun was lower in the West and the mountain chill had set in. Lawrence pointed to a table under the trees.

'That's where I write when the weather's good,' he said.

He had just finished the proofs of *The Plumed Serpent*, his Mexican book.

'It gives me a queer feeling, that country,' he said. 'Something dark and evil and full of old vindictive gods.'

NOTES

Kyle S. Crichton, American author and journalist, wrote the short memoir from which an extract is given above in 1950 or thereabouts. A shorter account of his interview with Lawrence at Taos had appeared in the New York newspaper *The World* on 11 October 1925.

1. Published in 1924.
2. Authoress and journalist; she was on the staff of the *English Review* and met Lawrence during his Croydon period. She was never in fact legally married to Hueffer.
3. Edward Garnett; see p. 78, n. 15.
4. Popular novelist who had known Lawrence since 1914. He portrayed Lawrence as Rayner in his novel *The South Wind of Love* (1937).
5. See p. 109, n. 14.
6. An incomprehensible error: Lawrence never visited Poland.
7. American authoress.
8. An American who acted as Lawrence's literary agent from 1921.

A Visit from Lawrence*

RICHARD ALDINGTON

[But, for] me, the great event of that year [1925] was the return of the Lawrences from America to the European scene. I had not seen them since 1919, and our correspondence had been extremely irregular. At one time Lawrence took a strong dislike to European things and people, and one heard only rumours of his wanderings to Ceylon and Australia and his settling in New Mexico. And now most surprisingly he wrote from London suggesting a meeting. I promptly wrote and invited the Lawrences for a long week-end, and in accepting Lawrence sent me some of his recent books which I had not read.

I had long admired Lawrence's work and, with sundry disagreements, liked him personally very much. But on reading these books and re-reading some earlier works I had, it seemed to me that I had hitherto under-rated him. Seven years' study of literature had sharpened my perceptions or, at least, taught me the rare accomplishment of how to read a book. Seven years of experience had made me more and more discontented with the Olympian, impersonal, and supposedly objective critical attitude adopted by *The Times*. I was more and more inclining to Norman Douglas's opinion that we should take up an author with the implied question: 'What has this fellow to say to *me*?' and give him the fairest chance of saying it. Lawrence seemed to have a good deal to say to me, and I liked what he had to say all the more because he went his own way so perkily.

The visit began a little inauspiciously, as Lawrence declared the cottage was 'sinister'. I can't imagine why, as it was sunny and full of books, with bright curtains and a smiling head of Voltaire over the piano; and the garden was brilliant with late summer flowers. And then I had forgotten that in the Midlands you show your respect to a guest by loading the high-tea table with enough provisions to stuff a dozen policemen; so Lawrence was greatly offended by my modest and wineless meal. All this was happily settled by a bottle of whisky for him to have a hot toddy at bedtime, a habit of his which was new to me and had apparently been acquired in America. After that he was in the best of spirits and good humour for the remainder of his stay.

As I knew he was contemplating a book on the Etruscans,[1] I had a dozen

---

* From *Life for Life's Sake* (New York: Viking Press, 1941) pp. 301–6.

standard works on the subject sent down from the London Library; and we spent a good deal of time turning them over and discussing Etruria, which was very important at that time in Lawrence's private mythology. We went for walks, and it was fascinating to see how quick he was in noticing things and making them interesting. Yet he could be devastating in his judgements of human beings. A neighbour of ours, an intellectual climber, had begged to be allowed a glimpse of him, and we contrived some excuse for a brief meeting. After she had gone Lawrence merely said: 'Dreary little woman.' I liked him for that, for I was sick of the way the London literati would suck up to the humblest of avowed or potential admirers. It would have been just the same if she had been the most potent of salon-rulers.

In private talks Lawrence and I agreed that so far as we were concerned something had gone wrong with England, our England, so that we felt like aliens in our own home. The only thing to do, Lawrence insisted, was to get out and stay out. In Mexico he had felt he ought to make one more attempt to fit into English life, but already he saw it was impossible, and was planning to go away and never return. (He went, and never did return.) He was evidently pining for his New Mexico ranch, for he talked of it constantly and with a nostalgic regret which made me quite unhappy on his behalf. But meanwhile before everything crashed—and he was intuitively certain it would crash sooner or later—we must have just a *little* more of Italy. Soon it would be *vendemmia*.[2] As we talked I saw so vividly the pinewoods and the olive gardens and the vineyards of the Florentine *contrada*, the great cream-white Tuscan oxen, with their wide horns and scarlet muzzle shields against flies, slowly dragging the big tubs of grapes to the press, the men and women singing and laughing and joking as they gathered the big purple clusters, the men and boys dancing on the grapes to crush out the wine, the *vino santo* heating over an open fire, and smelled the air sweet and heavy with the scent of crushed grapes as the vintagers sat down to their evening soup and bread and wine...And yes, I said, I would come to Scandicci for *vendemmia*.

The English, he said, had become half-angels, half-idiots. And he made us laugh with stories of the half-angelic, half-idiotic things they had done to him in the past few days. As David Garnett truly says, Lawrence was a born copy-cat. He amused us by mimicking a dialogue between himself and a woman in the train who tried to lend him her copy of the *Daily Mirror*, and another between himself and an obsequious butcher-boy—'he thanked me for going through the gate'. Curious that Lawrence, who was such a good satirist in conversation, was a comparatively poor one in writing. The reason is, I think, that in talk his satire was mostly laughter, whereas in print he scolded.

Best of all perhaps were the evenings when we sang old English and German folk songs, according to the Laurentian custom, and Lorenzo and Frieda talked of their wanderings and adventures. There was a haunted look in Frieda's eyes when she spoke of Lawrence's illness in Mexico City, and of her dreadful experiences in getting him back to the ranch. Lorenzo, it appeared, refused to have a mosquito curtain, maintaining that if you muffled yourself up in the bedclothes, the mosquitoes couldn't get you. But, as thousands of mediaeval angels danced on the point of a needle, thousands of anopheles danced and fed on the tip of Lorenzo's nose; with the natural result of a smart attack of malaria, which in turn aroused his latent TB. At the height of his illness he insisted on returning to the ranch, and was held up at the frontier by immigration officers, and but for the prompt and humane intervention of the American Consul would probably have died there. I think that was the real reason why Lawrence never went back to the ranch he loved so much; he would not have been allowed to cross the frontier again.

Apart from this unhappy episode, their wandering adventurous life sounded wholly fascinating and rewarding. Most travellers fail to interest me in their experiences, especially if I haven't been to the places they talk about. But Lawrence had the remarkable gift—in his writing and especially in his talk—of evoking his experiences so vividly and accurately that his listeners felt as if they had been present themselves, with the supreme advantage of being gifted with Lawrence's unique perceptions. It would be useless for me to try to reproduce Lawrence's talk; first, because I can't remember his exact words and anything short of that would be a travesty; second, because he has luckily left written accounts of many of these experiences in his books and letters.

He talked of that primitive, ice-cold, remote village of Picinisco where he and Frieda almost froze to death (end of *The Lost Girl*); of their life in Sicily and the trip to Sardinia (*Poems, Letters*, Introduction to *Memoirs of MM*, and *Sea and Sardinia*); of Ceylon, with blood-curdling imitations of night noises from the jungle and satirical acting of an American friend[3] burning joss-sticks to Buddha (*Letters* and *Poems*); of Australia (*The Boy in the Bush, Kangaroo*); and of the ranch (end of 'St Mawr', last essay in *Mornings in Mexico, Letters*). Some of this was already published and I had read it; but much was either unpublished or unwritten. As he related these things, they became almost epic to his listners. So might the Ithacans have sat enraptured by the tales of wandering Odysseus. What was remarkable, I reflected, was Lawrence's immense capacity for experience and almost uncanny power of reliving it in words afterwards. Of all human beings I have known he was by far the most continuously and vividly alive and receptive. 'What man most wants is to be alive in the flesh', he wrote when almost on his deathbed; and certainly few men and women can have been so much 'alive in the flesh' as he was. To say that he enjoyed life intensely would be misleading, because the phrase inevitably suggests all the luxuries and amusements and gratifications Lawrence despised. And, on the other hand, Shelley's 'pard-like spirit, beautiful and swift'[4] is too abstract and ethereal. The truth was somewhere in between those extremities.

NOTES

Richard Aldington (1892–1962), novelist, poet, and critic, met Lawrence in 1914. He published *D. H. Lawrence: an Indiscretion* in 1925 and a biography of Lawrence, *Portrait of a Genius but...* in 1950; he was also co-editor of Lawrence's *Last Poems* (1932). The subject of the above account is a weekend visit by the Lawrences to Aldington's home in Berkshire in August 1926.

1. Lawrence's *Etruscan Places* was published posthumously in 1932.
2. Grape harvest.
3. Presumably Earl Brewster: see p. 159.
4. The self-description is from Shelley's *Adonais*.

A Literary Tea-party*

WILLIAM GERHARDI

At a literary tea party, where the most strenuously besieged person was Margaret Kennedy, just then resting on the laurels she had won with *The Constant Nymph*,[1] a curiously untidy person in a morning-coat, which bore evidence that he had put it on under protest, came up to me, with a very fetching grin on his face and a curiously girlish, hysterical voice. I guessed immediately that he was D. H. Lawrence. He at once conveyed to me his disapproval of nearly everybody else in the room, and this, coupled with his jolly sort of approval of my *Polyglots*[2] and a lot of advice as to what I should avoid as a writer, all proffered in the most cheerful way, surprised me agreeably, since I had imagined Lawrence to be a disgruntled individual. He told me I had an absolutely original humour; that I should eschew sentimentality like poison; and that he thought I displayed an uncalled-for fear of death. Though feeling that nothing could be more baleful for the natural development of my own talent than the influence of that great rough force contorted into soured rhetoric, I nevertheless said to him at once, feeling that the occasion demanded it: 'You're the only one we younger men can now look up to.' He lapped it up, grinning with an air which suggested that he agreed with me, and later remarked to someone how pleasant it was at last to have met an intelligent man.

Lawrence took me across the room to introduce me to his wife, who, interrupting her conversation with another woman, beamed at me very largely and said: 'What do you make of life?'

* From *Memoirs of a Polyglot* (New York: Alfred A. Knopf, 1931) pp. 224–9. A shorter version appeared in the *Saturday Review*, CLI (20 June 1931) pp. 893–4.

'Come, come,' said her husband.

Mrs Lawrence told me how intensely her husband admired my books. Lawrence qualified this. 'I liked the humour,' he said. He scribbled down his address on the back of a cigarette box. I was to come to tea the next day.

When I called, Lawrence himself opened the door. His satanic look was absent. In the sunlight his red-bearded face looked harrowed and full of suffering, almost Christ-like. There were a couple of women at tea who seemed to resent a little our man-to-man conversation. One woman even went so far as to show impatience at the dryness, to her, of our subject, when finally she rose to leave. This roused Lawrence's fury. He imitated her inflexions. 'The insolence of the bitch!' he said when she was gone. 'Imagining we're here to entertain her!' And he once more imitated her unmercifully; after which he relapsed again into a serene tone of voice appropriate to our subject-matter—immortality. I mentioned Tolstoy saying life was a dream, death the awakening. Lawrence shook his head. 'No,' he said, 'I don't see it like that.' And he explained, very gently, looking at me very kindly with a sort of Christ-like expression. 'You see,' he said, 'it's like this: in your inside...' And I looked very attentive, very coy.

Our discussion continued for several hours. Lawrence's idea of immortal life was not something which would start after death, but a living reality within us going on even now, all the time, though intermittently clouded over by the illusion of time. He grew enthusiastic. Anything true to its own nature, he declared, was immortal. And his eyes expressed a gleam of self-satisfaction, certainly not immortal. A cat bristling his fur, a tiger in his fierceness...He stopped, a little troubled. I nodded comprehendingly.

We talked of Katherine Mansfield and Middleton Murry, whom, Mrs Lawrence told me, they regarded as children to be helped out of their troubles. I regretted that Middleton Murry, so sensitive and outstanding a critic, should be himself devoid of any talent whatever; and D. H. Lawrence sneered: 'I should have thought it was the only thing he had.'

It was now dinner time, and Lawrence asked me to stay. Mrs D. H. Lawrence, when you first set eyes on her, is the type of woman to gladden your heart. A real German Hausfrau, you say to yourself, suits him down to the ground, the intellectual, incompetent husband! The reality, however, is the reverse of this. Mrs Lawrence dislikes housework; her husband excels in it. Lawrence, a beam on his face, which was like a halo, brought in the dishes out of the kitchen, with the pride of a first-class chef in his unrivalled creations: no, as if cooking and serving your guests were a sacrament, a holy rite. When I told Lawrence of my friendship with Beaverbrook,[3] he astonished me by the intensity of his depreaction. Why should I allow myself to be patronised? Why should I, a messenger of the spirit, acknowledge Caesar? I, on the other hand, urged that the Holy Ghost in me prompted me to treat Caesar with that extra grace which the spirit can so easily lavish on the flesh—providing always that Caesar does not take unto himself that which is not Caesar's. But Lawrence demurred. If I wanted money, why not write articles for the magazines? He sat down and there and then wrote me a letter to Lengel of the *Cosmopolitan*. Authors, he implied, had been known to get on without the boosting of newspaper proprietors. 'And even with it,' I said. 'But why see any harm in the genuine interest in me of a charming newspaper proprietor, himself half a genius, who obviously cannot cherish an ulterior motive in regard to me?'

'Because,' Lawrence insisted, 'he hates you.'

'Come, come,' I said.

'I don't say he hates you personally,' Lawrence contended. 'But these men, they're like vampires. When they see an immortal soul they hate it instinctively.' His eyes gleamed. 'With a terrible black hatred, and instinctively try to annihilate what is immortal in you.'

At which remark Mrs Lawrence trembled with rage and expressed her agreement with some violence, which seemed to me a waste of effort, since if she had met Lord Beaverbrook she would undoubtedly have bowed to the man's extraordinary charm. D. H. Lawrence, wincing at this display of superfluous emotion, said quietly: 'Not so much intensity, Frieda.'

Mrs Lawrence, perhaps living up to the elemental naturalness of her husband's heroines, replied: 'If I want to be intense I'll be intense, and you go to hell!'

'I'm ashamed of you, Frieda,' he said. Whereupon Frieda's hatred for Lord Beaverbrook transformed itself into hatred for her husband, and was soon a spent cartridge.

I told Lawrence of some scientific difficulty I had about my plot for *Jazz and Jasper*.[4] I wanted a handful of people left on a mountain top with the rest of the world disintegrated to nothing. The problem had defeated H. G. Wells, who told me that the only plausible thing I could do was to make it a dream. D. H. Lawrence brushed aside the suggestion as unworthy and mapped the whole thing out for me in five minutes, breaking into ripples of girlish giggles at the ingenuity of his solution.

Lawrence said that the cells of Tchehov's writing were disintegrating cells, emitting, as they burst, a doleful twang which remained with us. Tolstoy's, on the contrary, were reintegrating cells, which gladdened the heart and tightened the nerves. When I told this to Middleton Murry, he sighed and said Lawrence never understood Tchehov. And I would add that, in my experience, I have never known anywhere, Russia not excepted, two souls more sensitively appreciative of Tchehov's work than Katherine Mansfield and Middleton Murry, though both could read him only in translation.

There was something so genuine and attractive about Lawrence, in spite of his curiously adolescent habit of derisive generalities, deploring the trend of his time, and other ballast of this kind, which he could have chucked overboard with advantage. Pointing to a crowd in the street, 'These London girls,' he said to me. 'I would as soon sleep with them as with a water closet.' And I pictured a number of attractive young girls, for no crowd is without them, mortified at the refusal of a sickly, red-bearded, untidy individual of middle-age to meet their advances, which in fact had not been forthcoming. 'I am fleeing again from my native country', in a letter. Sad, bad stuff! His being capable of it explains perhaps his readiness to surround himself with the most inconceivable mutts, patient listeners, haggard women, towards whom he no doubt conceived it his duty, at great effort—no wonder—to inculcate in himself a feeling of sex. And though he preached the gospel of the 'complete man', harmoniously attuned, Lawrence wore his red hair brushed down over the forehead, as if to conceal it—possibly to identify himself with the lowbrow primitive, whose centre of gravity is below the belt.

There was in Lawrence a real passion, a real longing to adjust his feelings about things to the enduring, the immortal side of life, intimated to us in fitful glimpses of Nature. Lawrence's revelation of animal life, his landscapes, and his human portraits are nearly always beautiful, original, powerful and moving. They are spoilt sometimes by needless reiteration prompted, one suspects, by a sort of gauche adolescent vanity—'I'll do it again, I will, if only to annoy you.' He is like a man who wants to show off his strength with a great big hammer and proceeds to drive the nails too far, and spoils the woodwork somewhat. Then testing it: 'It's strong', he says, and walks away swinging the hammer. Lawrence told me he liked his books while he wrote them, but hated them the moment he saw them in print. I am not surprised. His bitterness is the reaction of a proud spirit subjected from an early age to social and bodily humiliations. His inauspicious birth caused him to exert his strength fully as a rebel with little humour left to dispose of as a free man. Hence his hatreds, his insistence on his needs of 'blood contact' with the lower classes, as if it were not the inadequacy of all human contacts which throws one back on oneself, and makes the artist. Social self-consciousness, when it becomes articulate and tries to explain and justify itself, is a nuisance.

Everything I told Lawrence about the writers I had met seemed to provoke a kind of savage satisfaction in him, a grunt confirming his worst suspicions about the man. But when I mentioned Shaw, the passion and indignation which inspired his remarks evaporated completely. He said, with a disdain which did not pay Mr Shaw the compliment of being positive, a mere absence of interest, a mere negative: 'Are you interested in sociology? I'm not!'

With all his cheerful simplicity, his strength, his instinctive preoccupation with the real meaning of life (which is to 'evade', as Tchehov says, 'to circumvent, the unreal, the shallow, gratuitous, phantom-like which prevents us from being happy') there was withal something superfluous, something gawky and left-handed about Lawrence. His humour was defective. Yet, like so many people whose humour is poor, he prided himself on his tremendous sense of fun. 'I wish,' he wrote to me 'we created a *Monthly Express*, out of our various anatomies, to laugh at it all. Just a little magazine to laugh a few things to death. "The Big Toe Points out the Point or Points in Point Counter Point"—and so on. Let's make a little magazine, where even the liver can laugh.'⁵ Hardly first-rate.

It is not perhaps what a writer sees that matters in the end, but the 'smell' he exudes. Zola also thought he saw the truth and that it needed saying. Where is Zola's 'truth' to-day? Where Lawrence's 'truth' will be to-morrow. One writer's 'truth' is in the end as problematic as another's. It's the taste, the smell of his writing, which matter. And I cannot help thinking that D. H. Lawrence has a 'smell' about him which is unsatisfactory.

NOTES

William Gerhardi (born 1895), novelist. The meeting described took place on 23 October 1925, according to a letter written by Lawrence three days later (*Letters*, p. 640).

1. Highly successful novel published in 1924.
2. *The Polyglots*, a novel by Gerhardi published in 1925.
3. Politician and newspaper proprietor; at this time he controlled three leading London newspapers.
4. Published in 1928.
5. The joke, such as it is, is at the expense of Beaverbrook's *Daily Express* and *Sunday Express* and Aldous Huxley's novel *Point Counter Point* (1928).

Reminiscences: 1923–8*

BARBARA WEEKLEY BARR

In the winter of 1923–4, Elsa and I met Lawrence again. It may have been Catherine Carswell who had something to do with it, because her house in Hampstead was the meeting place. Middleton Murry was there that evening as well.

My childhood feeling about Lawrence had been that he was a fairly ordinary young man. This encounter gave me a very different impression altogether. I had not seen anyone like him before; nor have I since. He was tall and fragile—a queer, unearthly creature. He had a high-pitched voice, a slight Midlands accent, and a mocking, but spirited and brilliant

* From 'Memoir of D. H. Lawrence', in *D. H. Lawrence: Novelist, Poet, Prophet*, ed. Spender, pp. 9–10, 19–25, 25–7, 29–30.

manner. I liked his eyes. They were blue, wide apart, in cave-like sockets, under a fine brow. But they could be soft, and were kindly in the extreme. He had high cheekbones, a clubby Midlands nose, and a well-shaped jaw. His skin and hair were fair, and his beard red. When he was excited, or looking well, his cheeks had a delicate colour. He seemed beyond being human and ordinary, and I felt at once that he was more like an element— say a rock or rushing water. Lawrence talked to Elsa and me with great friendliness. Secretly I much preferred Middleton Murry, who sat near, dark, smiling and inscrutable, but more like the other men we had known.

Lawrence had just come back from America. 'Why is everyone over here so kind and loving?' he enquired derisively. 'If I get the porter to carry my bag, he wants to love me as well! I don't like it.' I thought Lawrence a queer fish.

In Hollywood, he told us, a friend had taken him to the house of a famous British film star. This man had made a typical entry into the gorgeous lounge, dressed in a sort of polo outfit, accompanied by baying dogs. In a few minutes the wife appeared, prettily leading their two children. All three were groomed to perfection. Lawrence thought the actor a buffoon. Hollywood he described as a huge lunatic asylum.

Frieda was lighthearted that evening, Murry a little embarrassed, and Lawrence very friendly. But Elsa and I did not know what to make of him. He talked to me about my art school, but was highly critical of it—and of me. Shortly afterwards, he remarked to Elsa, 'Barby is not the stuff of which artists are made.'

In February 1924, when he and Frieda went to visit her mother in Germany, Lawrence said of us to our grandmother: 'They are just little suburban nobodies'.

By the time Lawrence and Frieda had returned from America the second time (30 September 1925), I had become engaged. I took the man to dine with them at Garland's Hotel, where they sometimes stayed. He was considerably older than I was, a lazy, philandering sort.

In a black suit, looking frail and distinguished, Lawrence talked politely to the man. So did my mother. Afterwards we went to see *The Gold Rush*.[1]

It did not take Lawrence long to make up his mind about the engagement. 'We shall have to laugh her out of this,' he told Frieda. 'Where is Barby's *instinct*?' A little while after this I saw him at his sister Ada's[2] house at Ripley, just outside Nottingham. This was the first time Lawrence had a chance to talk to me about my 'young man'.

I met both his sisters there. Emily,[3] older than he, was a fair, stolid-looking Midlands type. Her husband, Sam, and she had not been getting on since he had been through the war, though at first they had been a devoted pair. Lawrence had been lecturing Emily in an effort to act as peacemaker.

Ada, the other sister, was two or three years younger than Lawrence.

She was a handsome, dark version of Lawrence and had a rather unhappy adoration for him.

When I saw my mother in this house, I thought she seemed a little out of place. I do not think Ada ever liked her, or forgave her for going off with her favourite brother.

Lawrence had a cold. Sitting up in bed in Ada's spotless room, he tálked to me about my 'young man'. 'You see,' he explained patiently, 'he hasn't enough *life*. Your father[4] with his books and so on has some life; this man hasn't *any*. The fight that every man knows he has to make against the world...he just shirks, using you as an escape from his life responsibility. He's a cadging dog, and he'll be much happier, really, if you kick him off...they always are. He's a bit inferior somehow. One feels a bit ashamed of him sneaking up the street.

'No, don't marry him, unless you feel divorce is a light business. Just shake him off, like a dog shakes off his fleas.'

I sat feeling woebegone during all this. To defend a weak position, I said, 'Well, he seems *stronger*, somehow, than I am.' It was a lie, and Lawrence looked mystified.

'"Stronger"? I simply don't see it,' he remarked, 'unless it is in being outside the pale...alien to society. Maybe he is in that way.' I began to be won over at this point. 'You can't play with life,' he told me. 'The only thing worth having, anyhow, is courage.'

Lawrence then came downstairs. We had a pleasant meal at Ada's. It was suggested that I should spend the night.

I telephoned my hostess, wife of a Nottingham professor. When she told her husband, he was very much alarmed. The idea of my spending a night under the same roof as Lawrence horrified him. Supposing he should happen to meet my father, who was in Nottingham, too? Presently his wife telephoned, imploring me to go back to their house. I reluctantly agreed and then went to tell the others.

Lawrence sprang to his feet, white with rage. 'These mean, dirty little insults your mother has had to put up with all these years!' he spat out, gasping for breath.

I was dismayed, not knowing how to act. The others were silent, Ada looking a little scornful.

Feeling something like a criminal, I crept dejectedly back to my Nottingham friends in the dark.

Lawrence and Frieda went abroad again a few days later, first to Baden, then on to Spotorno, in Italy.

In 1926, I spent a very happy spring with Lawrence and Frieda on the Italian Riviera.

This visit caused a certain amount of fuss and trouble at home, but eventually I reached Alassio, a few miles from the village of Spotorno, where they had rented the Villa Bernarda.

For reasons of family decorum, I was to stay at Alassio in a *pensione*, excellently managed by a Miss Hill and a Miss Gould. Miss Hill, a colonial and the niece of an archbishop, was romantic and ethereal. Miss Gould, a chubby Englishwoman doggedly devoted to Miss Hill, was a feminine replica of a vicar uncle of mine.

Lawrence came over with Freida to lunch and made himself very agreeable to the two spinsters. He rather liked taking a look at new people. 'One of those women's marriages,' he remarked amusedly afterwards.

Italy seemed a kind of paradise to me, though Alassio, once just a fishing village, had now become a sort of retreat for English gentlefolk living there to benefit from the favourable exchange rate. Many of them were Anglo-Indians—army people or civil servants—who looked on the Italians as a slightly improved kind of 'native'.

I tried to paint at Alassio and once when I was working out of doors, an English admiral came up, admired my painting, and took me out to tea.

Lawrence disapproved of this escapade. There was a curious streak of conventionality in him which cropped up now and then and which he no doubt inherited from his hardworking, puritanical mother. 'You want to be very careful of that kind of man,' he warned me severely.

He was also shocked to hear that I travelled third class in Italy and said, 'An English girl doing that here gives the impression that she is looking for an "adventure".' Fortunately, I was able to assure him that my worst experience had been drinking out of a bottle which was handed round a compartment by Italians with the friendly invitation 'Come on, don't be fussy.'

Before long I went to stay at the Villa Bernarda at Spotorno.

I remember so well walking in darkness up the narrow streets of the village, enthralled by its romantic ancient feeling and the wonderful foreign smell.

From the villa, a little way up the hill, I saw the light of an upstairs balcony window shine out towards the sea. The house was in two storeys, connected by an outside stone staircase. Built on a slope, the villa had a still lower part, intended for storing wine and oil.

When I knocked, Freida flung the door open joyfully. I saw Lawrence sitting up in bed against the sitting room wall.

'Why did you come so late?' he asked, crossly.

Talking endlessly over the chicken, which she had cooked on the charcoal fire, and the red wine, Freida and I were very happy. Lawrence, in his nearby bed, took in every word. I went to bed in one of the downstairs rooms.

The next morning I was awakened by loud bumping noises overhead. I was half prepared for this, as I had heard that the Lawrences threw saucepans or plates at each other. However, I hurried upstairs to intervene.

Freida, her neck scratched, was in tears. 'He has been horrid,' she said with a glare at the glum, pale man sitting on the edge of his bed. She had told him that, now I was with her at last, he was to keep out of our relationship and not interfere. This had infuriated Lawrence. I was exhilarated, rather than shocked.

It soon blew over, but a few days later the sparks flew again when Lawrence, after inveighing bitterly against Frieda, flung his wine in her face. This time I joined in, shouting, 'She's too good for you; it's casting pearls before swine!'

After Frieda had gone out of the room in anger, I asked Lawrence, 'Do you care for her?'

'It's indecent to ask,' he replied. 'Look what I've done for your mother! Haven't I just helped her with her rotten painting?'

In spite of his independent mind, Lawrence felt the need of sympathy. He was trying to sort out his feelings and values, and find a balance. He wanted Frieda to do the same, but she resisted him, somehow.

'Why does your mother want to be so *important*?' he demanded. 'Why can't she be simple and talk to me naturally, as you do, like a woman?'

I listened to his complainings. The incident was trivial, but his feeling seemed really shattered.

Afterwards when someone told me that he had said, 'Frieda's daughter tried to flirt with me', I thought it mean of him.

He and I liked to go for long walks. At Spotorno, and afterwards at Scandicci, we often went off in the afternoons and walked up the mountains. We talked a lot, mostly about people. Then we would forget about them, and just enjoy looking at the lovely Italian scene.

I began to paint the landscape. Lawrence, who had learned how to paint in oils, perhaps from Dorothy Brett in New Mexico, was a discerning critic. At first he was disparaging about my 'studio stuff'. '*Play* with the paint,' he urged me. 'Forget all you learned at the art school.'

One day, after spending the morning up the mountain, I came in and flung down a canvas despondently. 'It's good...there's air in it,' said Lawrence, jumping up. His judgement was sound, for this was the first picture I sold when I got back to London.

'Screw the tops on your paint-tubes afterwards,' Lawrence said. 'It just takes courage. You'll never get a husband if you are too untidy.'

Sometimes he took a hand in my painting, putting figures of peasants in the landscape, saying that it needed them to give it life. A picture of mine called *Peasants Building a House* was the most successful of these. Lawrence put in a black-haired young man drinking out of a Chianti bottle, and an old man holding a trowel, standing up in the half-built house.

The creative atmosphere of the Lawrence household was like a draught of life to me. I painted away assiduously at Spotorno.

'She might be an artist if she finds herself,' Lawrence told Frieda.

Sometimes he talked of his childhood, proudly saying that there had been more life and richness in it than in any middle-class child's home. Ada was his favourite sister. When they has been youngsters, he had once said to her, 'Let's go away, and find a better life together somewhere.' But Ada had been too timid; not having his gifts, she had perforce to stay where she was.

Lawrence had formerly hated his drunken father, but at this time had swung in sympathy towards him, away from his mother. She had been a sensitive woman, who, added to her hard lot, had endured the extra strain of having a self-indulgent, violent man as her husband.

When Lawrence was sixteen, he had a serious illness. His mother could not afford the medicines he needed, or even good food. This illness probably sowed the seed of the tuberculosis which killed him.

His mother died in her fifties of cancer, a disease Lawrence told me was 'usually caused by fret'.

I believe the Lawrences had some Irish blood in them. There was a story, too, that as a child his great-grandfather had been found wandering on the field of Waterloo after the battle, and brought home by English soldiers.

His elder sister Emily would recite sentimental poetry at great length to Lawrence when he was small. 'I used to pull her hair till she cried, but she went on and on, the tears streaming down her face.' He chuckled. So did I. I could just picture the plain Midlands face of the persistent, weeping Emily.

In the grounds of the Villa Bernarda were the ruins of an old castle. The villa itself was a haphazard sort of house. You could sit upstairs or downstairs and do as you pleased.

One afternoon, Lawrence was downstairs reading the autobiography of Mabel Dodge Luhan.[5]

'It's terrible, the will to power of this kind of woman,' he exclaimed. 'She destroys everybody, herself included, with her really frightful kind of will.' The manuscript seemed to fascinate him with horror. 'Read it, and let it be a lesson to you!' he said.

Lawrence must have read a great deal, though I did not often see him with a book. The only serious writer I heard him speak of with respect was Hardy. He didn't like Dickens, and said his people were 'frowsty'. Charlotte Brontë repelled him. He thought *Jane Eyre* should have been called *Everybody's Governess*. At that time he had just read *Gentlemen Prefer Blondes*[6] with amusement. The part about Germans and eating reminded him of my German grandmother.

'Two hours after supper she has a few snails. Then at bedtime some honeycake, with Schnapps. Really, I don't know *how* she can do it,' he told us, laughing.

Lawrence had been learning Russian, and would often turn up with a Russian dictionary. For some time he had wanted to visit Russia, believing there was a spark there which had been quenched in the rest of Europe. 'It seems to sink into a soupy state—Europe today,' he said. 'That's why I would like to be back at the ranch.'

Lawrence detested Bolshevism. Fascism was not to his taste either. While we were at Spotorno, an Englishwoman, Violet Gibson, shot at Mussolini. The Italians referred politely to the incident to us, and seemed almost sympathetic to the 'poor mad lady', whose bullet had passed through the cartilage of their bovine dictator's nose.

'Put a ring through it,' Lawrence advised a lieutenant of the Bersaglieri who happened to visit us the next day.

Some of *Mornings in Mexico* was written at the Villa Bernarda. In it he mentions Giovanni, the gardener who lived in the lower part among his chickens and wine bottles. Lawrence was indulgent towards the old man, but Frieda and I didn't care for him, because he would get drunk and frighten us.

Lawrence hardly ever wrote for more than four or five hours a day. His writing flowed off the end of his pen. 'If it doesn't, my writing is no good,' he said. He never discussed his writings with me, and advised me not to read his books till I was older. 'By the time you are forty, you will be able to understand them.' After Lawrence had finished a novel, he seldom wanted to look at it again.

Lawrence was quite clever with his hands. He could cook, sew, and was even good at embroidery.

In early February, my sister Elsa came for a brief visit. She flew to Paris, then still quite an enterprising thing to do. Lawrence was surprised that anyone should want to fly. 'I hate those artificial sensations,' he commented.

Elsa was better disciplined. Unlike me, she hated 'rows'. At the Bernarda she lectured Frieda about them, being concerned to see, after one of their quarrels, that Lawrence had tears in his eyes, a rare thing for him.

Elsa liked Spotorno, and joined in our afternoon walks, but more in disagreement with us than in accord. 'You and Lawrence encourage each other to be spiteful about everyone,' she said. There was some truth in this, though Lawrence thought that I was much worse than he was.

'You always have vendetta against someone,' he exclaimed one day. 'I wouldn't marry you, Barby, if you had a million pounds.' 'You'll never care about anybody,' he told me another time. 'You with your everlasting criticisms! If the Archangel Gabriel came down from Heaven and asked you to marry him, you'd find fault.' The idea seemed to amuse him.

One day he talked to Elsa about the stars, the millions of other universes, and the endlessness of space, saying, 'So you see our little lives aren't so very important after all.'

This reminder of human insignificance must have made Elsa reckless, because that evening she drank too much wine at supper, and talked wildly.

Seeing her tipsy, and listening to her haranguing Lawrence, I laughed hilariously, as did Frieda. Lawrence was amused too, but with reservations. 'The contrast from her usual self is too sharp, it frightens me,' he observed fastidiously.

Also in February, Lawrence's sister Ada came with a friend to stay at the Bernarda, so Elsa and I moved to the tiny Hotel Ligure. As we breakfasted on the balcony over the sea, Frieda appeared looking angry and upset. Ada and the friend had been 'bossy', she said. They had tried to oust her from her kitchen, where she managed so well.

Elsa and I both gave her advice. The situation disturbed us. When I went up to the Villa, I was very chilly to Ada.

'I don't trust Barby; she's too clever,' Lawrence told my mother resentfully. His feelings were hurt as well. The atmosphere was unpleasant for a few days until Lawrence went off to Florence with Ada, later going on alone to Rome and Capri where he stayed with the Earl Brewsters.

When he returned from his journey, Lawrence told me: 'Ada depresses me; I have to get away. She doesn't *believe* in me. She loves me…oh, yes!' Young then, and enthusiastic, I believed in him.

Lawrence thought that Elsa had more sense than I had. 'She is wise, and will make the best of life,' he wrote to me once. 'You are too inclined to throw everything away because of one irritating factor. There's been too much of that in all lives. You throw your soup at the waiter because it's too hot, or set fire to your bed, because there's a flea in it. Well, then can you lie on the ground.'

There was a quality in Elsa that he liked. Beyond her conventional autocratic exterior, he found a wistfulness.

'She rather makes a man feel he would like to put her in his pocket. Your pathos is unreal,' he said to me, discouragingly. 'Your troubles are all your own fault.'

Towards the latter part of April, Elsa and I were returning to England. Before we left Italy, Lawrence and Frieda took us to see Florence where we stayed at the Pensione Lucchesi, on the Arno. Lawrence showed us round Florence. At the Uffizi we stood in front of Botticelli's *Venus Rising from the Sea*, which he said was full of air. It was true: the figure seemed to float in sea air.

*   *   *

The Lawrences' relationship had been an enigma to me, but Maria[7] made me see its significance. 'A great passion' was how she described it. 'Frieda is silly. She is like a child, but Lawrence like her *because* she is a child,' she said.

The Villa Mirenda on a hill at Scandicci, a few miles from Florence, was an old white house, more dignified than the Villa Bernarda.

Two large chestnut trees were in flower in front of it when I went there in the spring of 1927. (I also visited the Lawrences at the Villa Mirenda the following spring, 1928.) It had oil lamps, and a stove to light with pine logs in the evenings. There was a piano, hired from Florence, in the big whitewashed sitting room. The floor was covered with fine woven rush. On the wall hung the big *Holy Family* which Lawrence had painted on one of the canvases Maria Huxley had given him. His *Eve Re-entering Paradise* was in another room, as well as the *Nuns with the Gardener* and a picture of naked men among autumn willows. He painted many others as well. Later an exhibition was arranged at the Warren Gallery which so shocked the prigs that the pictures were removed by order of the Home Secretary.[8]

These paintings lacked what is called 'technique', but they were alive and mystical. They had a shiny surface like oleographs, caused by Lawrence sometimes smearing on the paint with his hands.

Lawrence was very pleased with his painting, which took less toll of him than writing. He said he was going to give up being an author and paint instead.

Frieda also painted occasionally. Her wonderful colour sense gave her pictures life and gaiety. One of them—of chickens at the ranch—she gave to Elsa, so I put it up on a mantelpiece at home.

'I say, I like that!' exclaimed my father. 'Who did it?'

Oh, someone or other...I forget,' I replied.

At the Villa Mirenda we sang the Hebridean songs, Frieda accompanying us. Lawrence sang in a high-pitched voice. It gave the songs a weird 'other-world' sound, which suited them, although orthodox musicians would no doubt have shuddered. In fact, an elderly friend who was with me on this visit—staying disconsolately at the inn—expressed her disapproval of such amateurish singing.

'What a conceited ass she is,' remarked Lawrence's Scots friend, Miss Millicent Beveridge,[9] who was there too.

We also sang *Red, Red Is the Path to Glory*, a tragic border song, and the *Lay of the Imprisoned Huntsman*, which Frieda liked to sing. Aunt Else told me that whenever she heard her sing it she felt sad, because there was a sound in Frieda's voice of a being also imprisoned.

One evening at Scandicci, a family of English puppet-makers named Wilkinson invited us to a party, where everyone was asked to do a 'turn'. The hostess, dressed as William Wordsworth, recited 'We Are Seven'. Lawrence, who had once seen Miss Florence Farr[10] in London, sat down at an imaginary harp, drew his hands across it, began 'I will arise and go now' in a falsetto voice, and ended it with a 'ping-a-ling'.

This take-off of the high-faluting was over the heads of the company. On the way home Lawrence raved at Frieda for having allowed him to do it.

Lawrence was aloof. He disliked too easy intimacy, or gatherings where people 'got together'. He said once that the idea of putting his arm round a woman's waist and dancing with her appalled him.

Pretension and commonness upset him. One could sometimes see a glimpse of the working-class Midlander, but he was always remote from vulgarity.

He could be cruel, and even nagging, but never callously indifferent. He did not have the ordinary man's domineering dependence on his womenfolk, but could mend, cook and find his own possessions.

Lawrence had the clean, fresh look of so many fair people. He liked old clothes, but never looked ill-kempt.

'I don't mind a bit of vanity,' he once remarked. He would advise us about our clothes, and was interested in our dressmaking attempts. 'Sew it properly,' he would implore us. 'Things can't keep their shape unless you do.'

I remember thinking that his advice about an orange jumper I was knitting at the Mirenda must necessarily be inspired. 'The only colour that goes with yellow is pink,' he insisted. So Frieda and I finished it off with a strawberry border.

Sometimes she and I sat on one of the little balconies of the upstairs salon, among the white chestnut flowers. There one afternoon we read the MS of another feminine autobiography—an English one this time—with wicked amusement.

'Now I have two women interfering with my papers,' protested Lawrence. Things like that did not really annoy him, though.

At this time his illness made further inroads. He was more frail than he had been at Spotorno, and increasingly irritated by the people around him. When Pietro, the young Italian who did the errands with his donkey cart, came into the kitchen of the Mirenda while English friends were there, Lawrence said, 'Here he comes, thinking he will give them a chance to see the interesting young peasant.'

The two little boys of the Mirenda cottage he really did like. One had large grey eyes. 'One sees those eyes like water among the Sicilians,' he told me. I longed to see those olive-skinned people with water eyes.

'That boy has a voice like a thrush, Lorenzo,' said Frieda delightedly.

'Yes, he has,' replied Lawrence in his quick way.

Scandicci was like Paradise in the spring, the Mirenda a house of magic. I loved my big whitewashed room which Frieda had arranged with her wonderful taste. After I had gone back to England, she wrote, 'Your ghost still lingers in your room.'

*   *   *

That spring [1928] in Scandicci, I could not, unfortunately, do any successful paintings. But I was never bored; with Lawrence life was always absorbing, even when he was out of humour. He was brilliantly penetrating, and in assessing human relationships had an uncanny gift.

'He will leave her,' he said of a young married pair. 'Some other woman will want him, especially if she sees he has a wife and child.' This proved true. He thought that in most people the psyche was 'double', loving on one side and betraying on the other. It was our modern malady, according to him.

When my sister Elsa was going to be married, Lawrence wrote to me, 'Don't let her marry a man unless she feels his physical presence warm to her.'

'I don't need Lawrence's advice,' Elsa told me.

In this letter he also said, I think, 'Passion has dignity; affection can be a very valuable thing, and one can make a life relationship with it.'

Unfortunately these letters were all lost.

'As for Barby,' he said one evening as we sat at supper by the lamplight, 'she will never finish anything, any relationship. If she marries, she won't finish her marriage either. I tell you, Frieda,' he said, in a sharp, devastating voice, 'she won't *finish* it!'

He went on: 'I don't know what will become of her, simply I don't. If her father goes on giving her three pounds a week, she is very lucky. No one ever gave me that.'

All this was very discouraging. But Frieda stuck up for me determinedly.

After I had gone back to London, and was drifting unhappily in the way that was becoming a habit with me, Lawrence wrote quite charitably, ending, 'Don't throw yourself away; you might want yourself later on.'

One day at the Mirenda we looked through an old Italian opera brochure. There was a photograph of a woman with rich dark hair piled on top. 'I wish women looked like that now,' Lawrence remarked. Another portrait was of a full-looking man with a big moustache. 'I should like to be that man. Yes, I really would like to be just like him,' he said wistfully

In their life together, Frieda must sometimes have suffered, and felt lonely. At first, many people had been hostile to her. Lawrence was inclined to be jealous, and would often sneer at the few friends she did have. The strain on her remarkable good humour must been colossal. She believed in him, though. He needed her belief, and was unhappy without her.

At this time she wanted to holiday by herself. I was going back to Alassio. She came too, and then went off alone.

Lawrence said to Maria Huxley, 'Frieda has changed since she went away with Barby.'

He did not reproach my mother. One evening at the Mirenda he said to her, 'Every heart has a right to its own secrets.'

NOTES

For a note on Barbara Barr see p. 90.
  1. Chaplin's film appeared in 1925.
  2. See p. 10.

3. Emily King, née Lawrence.
4. Professor Ernest Weekley, see p. 88.
5. See p. 171.
6. Anita Loos's successful novel appeared in 1925.
7. Maria Huxley.
8. In July 1929.
9. Scots painter who lived mainly in Paris: see *Letters*, pp. 514–15.
10. See p. 78, n. 13.

In Capri Again*

DOROTHY BRETT

'Let us go round by the cave,' I suggest.

'All right,' you reply, 'we will lunch on those rocks over there.' When we reach the rocks, we settle down and eat our sandwiches and drink our bottle of wine. We have a small bottle each of light red wine. We are sheltered from the wind and the sun is hot, but you look somewhat tired. You reach out and pick a flower, holding it tenderly in your hands.

'Do you know what this is, Brett?'

'No,' I answer, 'I don't.'

'Good Lord, Brett, what an ignoramus you are! Did you never study botany? It is the old Greek asphodel. Asphodel is so lovely a name, and the flower is lovely, too. One of the things I enjoyed most as a boy at school, besides drawing, was botany; and later, as a schoolmaster, the two things I liked teaching best were drawing and botany; and I had very good classes in both. You are lucky, Brett, in the things you have not had to do to earn your living.' Certain chapters in *The Rainbow* rushed into my mind. 'Yes,' you say, 'It can be very bad; but I never had much trouble. The boys, I think, liked me. But even when a boy, I always felt there was something so mean in tormenting one's teacher.'

*   *   *

While Achsah, you and I sit in the living room, waiting for supper, you talk of marriage quietly. There is something even more gentle and sensitive than usual about you this evening.

'Women,' you say, 'are hardly ever true to themselves; that is why they

---

* From *Lawrence and Brett*, pp. 264–5, 266–7.

are not true to others; that is what makes most of the tragedies of married life. Also women destroy themselves by their obsession to have their own way.' And you sigh, heavily, while Achsah and I look at each other over your head.

*   *   *

At supper, we talk of our various childhoods. You give a vivid and very terrible picture of your early life. 'It was terrible,' you say. 'Terrible, with the constant struggle, the lack, nearly, of the bare necessities of life. To be sick meant the doctor; that meant any extra shillings went for the doctor's fee and medicine; and usually we had only one shilling extra every week— only one. Think of that, Brett. Boots and clothes had to be saved up for slowly, week by week. Every little thing we needed extra, meant saving and scraping for, and not having enough to eat. And the wages varied— never more than twenty-five shillings a week, sometimes much less.

'At times my mother hardly knew what to do, how to manage. You do not know, Brett; you have never experienced certain things owing to your up-bringing; you never can know. My eldest brother died, I believe, because of those early days of semi-starvation, of never having enough clothes, enough warmth, enough to eat. He died of pneumonia, while overworking, and he was, I always think, even more brilliant than I am.'

We none of us say anything—we are too horrified. Then to some query of Earl's about Buddhism, about Oriental teaching, you reply:

'Eternity. My idea of Eternity, I can best illustrate by the rainbow: it is the meeting half way of two elements. The meeting of the sun and of the water produce, at exactly the right place and moment, the rainbow. So it is in everything, and that is eternal...the Nirvana...just that moment of the meeting of two elements. No one person could reach it alone without that meeting.' And you lapse into a long silence.

NOTE

For a note on Dorothy Brett see 201–2. During the winter of 1925–6, the Lawrences rented the Villa Bernardo at Spotorno, near Genoa (their landlord was Angelo Ravagli, who long afterwards became Frieda's third husband). In the spring of 1926 Lawrence went to Capri for a visit to the Brewsters, who were on the point of setting off again for the Far East; there he saw Dorothy Brett once more.

Lawrence as a Companion*

ALDOUS HUXLEY

My second meeting with Lawrence took place some years later, during one of his brief revisitings of that after war England, which he had come so much to dread and to dislike. Then, in 1925, while in India, I received a letter from Spotorno. He had read some essays[1] I had written on Italian travel; said he liked them; suggested a meeting. The next year we were in Florence and so was he. From that time, till his death, we were often together—at Florence, at Forte dei Marmi, for a whole winter at Diablerets, at Bandol, in Paris, at Chexbres, at Forte again, and finally at Vence where he died.

In a spasmodically-kept diary I find this entry under the date of December 27th, 1927: 'Lunched and spent the p.m. with the Lawrences. DHL in admirable form, talking wonderfully. He is one of the few people I feel real respect and admiration for. Of most other eminent people I have met I feel that at any rate I belong to the same species as they do. But this man has something different and superior in kind, not degree.'

'Different and superior in kind.' I think almost everyone who knew him well must have felt that Lawrence was this. A being, somehow, of another order, more sensitive, more highly conscious, more capable of feeling than even the most gifted of common men. He had, of course, his weaknesses and defects; he had his intellectual limitations—limitations which he seemed to have deliberately imposed upon himself. But these weaknesses and defects and limitations did not affect the fact of his superior otherness. They diminished him quantitively, so to speak; whereas the otherness was qualitative. Spill half your glass of wine and what remains is still wine. Water, however full the glass may be, is always tasteless and without colour.

To be with Lawrence was a kind of adventure, a voyage of discovery into newness and otherness. For, being himself of a different order, he inhabited a different universe from that of common men—a brighter and intenser world, of which, while he spoke, he would make you free. He looked at things with the eyes, so it seemed, of a man who had been at the brink of death and to whom, as he emerges from the darkness, the world reveals itself as unfathomably beautiful and mysterious. For Lawrence, existence

---

* From the Introduction to *Letters*, pp. xxix–xxxii.

was one continuous convalescence; it was as though he were newly reborn from a mortal illness every day of his life. What these convalescent eyes saw, his most casual speech would reveal. A walk with him in the country was a walk through that marvellously rich and significant landscape which is at once the background and principal personage of all his novels. He seemed to know, by personal experience, what it was like to be a tree or a daisy or a breaking wave or even the mysterious moon itself. He could get inside the skin of an animal and tell you in the most convincing detail how it felt and how, dimly, inhumanly, it thought. Of Black-Eyed Susan, for example, the cow at his New Mexican ranch, he was never tired of speaking, nor was I ever tired of listening to his account of her character and her bovine philosophy.

'He sees,' Vernon Lee once said to me, 'more than a human being ought to see. Perhaps,' she added, 'that's why he hates humanity so much.' Why also he loved it so much. And not only humanity: nature too, and even the supernatural. For wherever he looked, he saw more than a human being ought to see; saw more and therefore loved and hated more. To be with him was to find oneself transported to one of the frontiers of human consciousness. For an inhabitant of the safe metropolis of thought and feeling it was a most exciting experience.

One of the great charms of Lawrence as a companion was that he could never be bored and so could never be boring. He was able to absorb himself completely in what he was doing at the moment; and he regarded no task as too humble for him to undertake, nor so trivial that it was not worth his while to do it well. He could cook, he could sew, he could darn a stocking and milk a cow, he was an efficient wood-cutter and a good hand at embroidery, fires always burned when he laid them, and a floor, after Lawrence had scrubbed it, was thoroughly clean. Moreover, he possessed what is, for a highly strung and highly intelligent man, an even more remarkable accomplishment: he knew how to do nothing. He could just sit and be perfectly content. And his contentment, while one remained in his company, was infectious.

As infectious as Lawrence's contented placidity were his high spirits and his laughter. Even in the last years of his life, when his illness had got the upper hand and was killing him inchmeal, Lawrence could still laugh, on occasion, with something of the old and exuberant gaiety. Often, alas, towards the end, the laughter was bitter, and the high spirits almost terrifyingly savage. I have heard him sometimes speak of men and their ways with a kind of demoniac mockery, to which it was painful, for all the extraordinary brilliance and profundity of what he said, to listen. The secret consciousness of his dissolution filled the last years of his life with an overpowering sadness. (How tragically the splendid curve of the letters droops, at the end, towards the darkness!) It was, however, in terms of anger that he chose to express this sadness. Emotional indecency always shocked him profoundly, and, since anger seemed to him less indecent as an emotion than a resigned or complaining melancholy, he preferred to be angry. He took his revenge on the fate that had made him sad by fiercely deriding everything. And because the sadness of the slowly dying man was so unspeakably deep, his mockery was frighteningly savage. The laughter of the earlier Lawrence and, on occasion, as I have said, even the later Lawrence was without bitterness and wholly delightful.

Vitality has the attractiveness of beauty, and in Lawrence there was a continuously springing fountain of vitality. It went on welling up in him, leaping, now and then, into a great explosion of bright foam and iridescence, long after the time when, by all the rules of medicine, he should have been dead. For the last two years he was like a flame burning on in miraculous disregard of the fact that there was no more fuel to justify its existence. One grew, in spite of constantly renewed alarms, so well accustomed to seeing the flame blazing away, self-fed, in its broken and empty lamp that one almost came to believe that the miracle would be prolonged, indefinitely. But it could not be. When, after several months of separation, I saw him again at Vence in the early spring of 1930, the miracle was at an end, the flame guttering to extinction. A few days later it was quenched.

NOTES

For a note on Aldous Huxley see p. 123.
  1. Published as *Along the Road* in 1925.

A Visit to the
Villa Mirenda*

OSBERT SITWELL

I only met Lawrence once, when he and his wife were living in Tuscany. I was staying near by and they asked my sister and myself to have tea with them; so we drove through the blossoming countryside—for it was high May—to his farmhouse. This square, blue-painted house stood among gentle hills, with rather Japanese pines springing from rocks and brown earth in the distance, and with the foreground sprinkled with bushes of

* From 'Portrait of Lawrence', *Penny Foolish* (London: Macmillan, 1935) pp. 296–7.

cistus, flowering in huge yellow, white and purple paper roses. A few cypresses, the most slender of exclamation-marks—not robust, as they are further south—orchestrated the landscape. Lawrence opened the door to us, and it was the first time I had ever realised what a fragile and goatish little saint he was: a Pan and a Messiah; for in his flattish face, with its hollow, wan cheeks, and rather red beard, was to be discerned a curious but happy mingling of satyr and ascetic; qualities, too, which must really have belonged to him, since they are continually to be found in his work. It was, certainly, a remarkable appearance. Unlike the faces of most geniuses, it was the face of a genius.

He was extremely courteous, I remember, and prepared the tea himself, doing all the work: which grieved one, for he looked so ill. The rooms were charming, simple, Italian-farmhouse rooms, with none of that broken, gold junk one so frequently encounters in the homes of the English in Italy; a great relief. On the other hand, they were hung with large canvases by Lawrence: pictures that he had just at that period begun to paint. These, though many wise people have since praised them, I thought then—and still think—crudely hideous and without any merit save that he painted them and in so doing may have rid himself of various complexes, which might otherwise have become yet more firmly rooted in his books; useful, then, but not beautiful.

Two hours, two extremely delightful hours, we spent with them, and then he saw us off at the door, standing with the evening sun pouring down on that extraordinary face: but Lawrence, I am sure, must always have been glad to be alone once more. I left Italy a day or two later, and never saw him again, so that, scarcely knowing him, I am left to fit those two hours and their impressions on to that solitary, delicate and ever so interesting figure.

NOTE

Sir Osbert Sitwell (1892–1969), English writer. The sister referred to is Dame Edith Sitwell, poetess (1887–1964). Although Sir Osbert states that this encounter in May 1927 was his only meeting with Lawrence, David Garnett (*Flowers of the Forest*, p.190) recalls seeing him and his brother Sacheverell, together with Lawrence and Frieda, among the company at Gordon Square on 11 November 1918 (see also *Letters*, pp. 531–2, 754).

Illness*

ACHSAH BREWSTER

A year had passed without our seeing the Lawrences. It was May of 1928: they had offered us their Florentine villa, the Mirenda, for the summer, and we had gone there to see them before they left for the French Alps. As usual at that season the poppies were in full glory. The little hills gambolled together as for a Bennozzo Gozzoli picture. When we saw Lawrence we suddenly realised that he was very ill, and knew that we must not postpone to the future our time with him, but seize each passing day. He was fastidiously dressed in white flannels with a flax-blue coat. (It became customary with him to wear such a coat).

He led us from room to room showing us the walls adorned with his paintings. Their sensitive colour and tactile qualities, their ease of technique and their spontaneity and their expressiveness pleased me. In the living-room hung at one end the *Holy Family*; in the dining-room was the *Scene from Boccaccio*, in Frieda's room was his *Pieta* and in Lawrence's room was a painting of nude figures with beasts snarling around; I do not remember what he called it but to me it was the hounds of heaven! I enjoyed the picture of early spring with glowing willow trees and nude figures.

The next day while we were there a group of three men arrived, among them Norman Douglas. (I believe it was their first meeting since their disagreement over the publication of *Memoirs of the Foreign Legion*.)[1] Lawrence was a dignified host. The jovial Douglas talked voluble German with Frieda. Lawrence looked pale and wan beside them.

It was decided that we should go to the Alps with Frieda and Lawrence, instead of remaining at the villa. The trip began to have a lure.

Our farewell luncheon was gay. The train journey was an adventure. As we sped along, the passengers descended one after another, until by night we had our compartment to ourselves with the adjoining ones empty. Then we began to sing hymns. Lawrence knew all the Moody and Sankey revival songs, the Salvation Army tunes, every word of all the verses. One followed another in growing dramatic effect, until the climax was reached in *Throw out the life-line*. He stood up and threw out an imaginary lasso to the drowning souls, hauling them in strenuously. But the exhilaration from

* From *D. H. Lawrence: Reminiscences and Correspondence*, pp. 281–5.

singing did not keep Lawrence from being tired when we reached Turin, where we decided to spend the night. The next morning a glorious magnolia blossom was placed on our luncheon table in the sun. It opened out full even as we watched it—a thrilling spectacle of a flower's response to the sun.

There was no definite notion of where we were going, only the pleasure of exploring. We thought the Savoy Alps with the sight of Mount Blanc might be what we wanted.

Our next stop was Chambéry. Early in the morning Frieda and Lawrence were up and had returned from a tour of the town, having investigated the shops, bringing back an orange cravat for Earl, before the rest of us were out. Lawrence was in a holiday mood.

How happy we felt in Aix-les-Bains. The hotel verandahs filled with gay groups dining in the open enchanted us as did the long menus. He read the list with gusto, electing fresh brook trout and grilled chicken. While he scrunched the bones of these viands he made derogatory remarks about our soufflé and salads. Two waiters vied with each other to serve us. There was bickering between them throughout the meal. When coffee was served the dark waiter gave a resounding smack full in the face of his colleague, whose cheek turned from rose to scarlet. Frieda decided it was misled patriotism, but Lawrence was grievously disturbed and felt it was a profound cosmic discord!

It was Lawrence who found the first lilies-of-the-valley; to be sure he only found them in the flower-market, but they were wild ones. We were on our way to the lake, which seemed an interminable distance, and when we arrived there we sank down in a daze of weariness, trying to refresh ourselves with tea served with eight varieties of jam, while we watched a swan career on the lake with two of her young tucked under her wings.

From Grenoble we motored up the heights to a sunny plateau, swung out over the valley, with a view of the snow-covered mountains. The mountain flowers were in their splendour; deep purple columbine, blue gentians, pansies, forget-me-nots, lilies-of-the-valley, alpine roses. A rustic inn was found in the floweriest spot of all, christened St Nizier-de-Pariset, and there we arranged to make a sojourn. On the following day we returned in high spirits to settle in.

Early in the morning, after our first night there, the proprietor knocked at Earl's door, announcing that monsieur had been ill in the night.

'Oh, no,' said Earl, 'I was not ill.'

'But not you, the other one—he coughed all night.'

He added that he was sorry not to be able to keep Lawrence, but there was no choice, since the law on that plateau prohibited his having guests with affected lungs. Monsieur would have to go.

Ill as Lawrence was he had never admitted to us the seriousness of his malady. He had continued to refer to it as an 'annoying' irritation of his bronchials. Never before had the doors of a hotel been closed to him because of it.

Shocked and dismayed, we had to break this news to Frieda, whom it upset still more. It was decided not to tell Lawrence what had happened. Although the evening before we had all agreed enthusiastically that the place was *'perfect'*, *'entirely to our taste'*, *'a rare find'*, the inn-keeper *'remarkably fine'*—we now decided to tell Lawrence that we no longer liked it, and wanted to go away. *What* would he say to such a sudden change? To such fickleness of taste? We greatly wondered.

Lawrence seemed not in the least surprised, and replied quite calmly — that strangely enough he couldn't bear the place either, that he had awakened in the morning not wanting to stay. 'There was something *mingy* about that inn-keeper. I felt it from the first.'

Did he suspect what had happened? We never knew. But all day he kept repeating: 'Curious how I hated that place!'

NOTES

For a note on Achsah Brewster see p. 165.
  1. See p. 157, n. 4.

Île de Port-Cros*

BRIGIT PATMORE

[In October–November 1928 the Lawrences spent a month on Île de Port-Cros, off the Mediterranean coast of France; they stayed there with Richard Aldington, who had rented a house from Jean Paulhan, editor of the *Nouvelle Revue Française*.]

They arrived on a morning to match paradise, but we were saddened at once by the unexpected, dreadful weakness of Lorenzo. The long walk up from the tiny harbour had certainly been too much for him, but there was no way of avoiding this over-exertion, for no cars were allowed on the island, and not even a horse-drawn vehicle could pass over the huge stones encumbering the path at certain corners.

But Lawrence never complained: he seemed to approve the place, its loveliness and quiet, and being with friends with whom he could say what he liked and do as he pleased.

*From 'Conversations with Lawrence', *London Magazine*, IV, pp. 38–43.

The Paulhans had left an Italian boy, Giuseppe, to do all the work except cooking. He had a donkey called Moses: the two of them went down into the valley to draw fresh water and then fetch provisions from the one shop down by the harbour. This reminded Lorenzo of his beloved Italy: it amused him to see the little donkey browsing and tiny chickens pecking around his four feet.

Frieda and Arabella shared the more serious cooking of luncheon and dinner and I looked after breakfasts—'Because you don't mind getting up early, do you?'—but I think they mistrusted my power to do anything less simple.

Lorenzo had his breakfast in bed. So, about quarter to seven on those shining autumn mornings, when light itself was a flower perfumed like a god's wine, I used to carry a tray across the courtyard to his room. I'd knock and cry 'Can I come in?' then plunge right in so as to save him calling out through the heavy door.

'Hello, darling. Hope you want your *lovely* breakfast!'

He was always awake and his eyes smiled, but he seemed terribly exhausted, and while putting a coat round his shoulders I could feel his pyjamas soaked with perspiration. However it was against the rules to suggest that anything was wrong.

'What do you bet I've forgotten this morning?'

'Nothing. Giuseppe's got a good memory.'

'Him! You should have seen the tray he laid. Looked like a stonemason's dinner pail. Don't know how he managed it with all Madame Paulhan's pretty Galeries Lafayette do-das.'

'What's this!'

It was a triumph to have roused his interest.

'Oh just a little bit of bacon. Real old Irish, I believe. This flower to match your coat grows down the cliff under your window.'

It had taken a week's plotting and correspondence to get that bacon. He seemed rather wistful for English food and this wrung our hearts. One was expected on the island to live on spaghetti, and strange miniature monsters from the sea, and wine: as Lawrence never drank wine, which is necessary to make a diet of *pasta* endurable, something had to be done about it.

'Here's your notebook and pencil—or do you want your fountain pen? Here's the bell. Ring like mad if you want more hot water, although I'm coming over again in a minute and you can think out your orders.'

But he never had any orders. No man ever wanted less waiting on. Whenever I heard a faint shout of 'Brigit' and ran to his window overlooking the courtyard, he would say something like—'Do ask Richard if one can use the word "Catasto" in Italian for "tithe" or is it more exactly "tax".'

For amusement Lawrence was translating an early Italian story called 'Dr Manente'[1] and this led to lively discussions between him and Richard on technical points. Typing of the manuscript was given to me and I had to do the last page four or five times. Lorenzo inexplicably became fussy about the shape of the lines, the last word had to shrink into an inverted peak right in the middle of the page. For a few morning hours he would sit up in bed and write in a clear sloping script which was blissfully easy to read. The Viking Press had asked him for a short essay on the censorship of books and in less than an hour he wrote his lucid exposition on the inner cover of a book. It needed no corrections. His mastery always roused my amazement; it was the same with subtler thoughts. After his death, when I was in Florence, Orioli asked me to correct the proofs of *The Apocalypse*.[2] There were three versions in notebooks to be gone through but the alterations were slight, just the rejection of words which seemed superfluous.

A more unique trait was that he never minded being interrupted while writing—no glare of hatred from frenzied rolling eye met the intruder. Knowing this I often told him what was happening outside the fort. He could go out so seldom and was amused to hear of the stray creatures that might wander up to our pinnacle.

One day I rushed up to his window: 'Darling, there's never been anything so lovely! There are *three* rainbows in the valley! Three!'

He had a hat on, a rakish Homburg at a cavalier angle, for the draughts from the tiny window at the bed's head sometimes whisked around fiercely. He simply looked up, smiled dreamily and said: 'There, there', and went on writing.

Laughing, I went back to the ramparts wondering if perhaps he hadn't yearned to curse me.

Without being too obvious we arranged that someone should always be at hand in case he was not well, for the fact that there was no doctor on the island worried us.

One sun-filled afternoon we were all sitting in the courtyard sheltered from any wind by thick, yellow cystus bushes. Lorenzo had his feet up on a chair, his knees covered with a sheepskin coat. Like most red-haired people his colour was intensified, yet more transparent, in the sunshine.

He was very gay, giving us through his imitations a gallery of portraits: it was a brilliant entertainment. Then the other three went off to bathe. It was mournful to see the expression in Lawrence's eyes: they watched Frieda until she disappeared through the door leading to the drawbridge. Richard's and Frieda's laughter came back to us. Lorenzo's eyes widened; I almost wished that Richard could have hidden his gaiety, and said: 'Richard hasn't been so carefree for years. It always goes to the head a bit.'

'That may be.' Then snappily, as if we were in a kindergarten: 'He can't live on his charm for ever.' Later he added: 'I don't know how it is I have no real men friends.'

'But several men I know are devoted to you. But you trample on their feelings.' He looked astonished.

'Well, I can't help it,' he said grimly, 'if these men who go to public schools can't face the truth. They're not in leading-strings even they're in strait-waistcoats, and they tie up their tongues and develop their biceps. You can't think or feel much with a bicep. Besides, they're not such sportsmen, they hit you when you're down, my lass, and don't you forget it!'

'Heavens! your pen has much more bite in it than their swords or fists—or whatever they use.'

'But you want to feel at one with your fellow-creatures...sometimes.'

'I don't know anyone who is more so than you.'

'No. Not with them. And they can go their own inferior blazes. Even their voices are emasculate. No wonder women are restless and hard. "A woman wailing for her demon lover" indeed! There's something for you to write about.' Then suddenly, 'Are you going to marry that boy back in England?'

'Of course not. I'm old enough to be his mother.'

'*That* doesn't matter. Young men now seem to want to marry their grandmothers.'

I was silent, so he went on:

'You know you're rather like the woman in *Rawdon's Roof*.³ I thought that as I was reading it last night. What do you think she did?'

'I don't know. But don't *you?*' He shook his head. 'It doesn't matter anyway. How witty that story is, so light the touch. Lorenzo, how wonderful it would be if you wrote a play now, turning to that side of you. Bits of *David*⁴ made one realise how easily you could. Rawdon with his "No woman shall sleep under *my* roof." It's unbitter, cool, soothing laughter.'

He was quiet for a few moments, and then:

'Yes. I know it's time for me to write something different, but I just don't feel interested.'

'Oh, why?'

He hesitated: 'When you think you have something in your life which makes up for everything, and then find you haven't got it...Two years ago I found this out.'

It was so final, the way he said this: he was away in a loneliness where nothing but what he desired could be of use to him. And what words would help? After some moments I said:

'When I was ill a few years back and had to begin living all over again I dreaded the effort. But from you I learnt...I would say to trees "oh tree give me your strength", to water and flowers "give me your soft brilliance". Your words taught me that and they helped.'

'Yes. Once I could do that. I can't any more.'

Giuseppe passed us with Moses and I went to get letters for the post. When I came back Lorenzo had disappeared. I wandered round a little grass-covered hill and stood on the western ramparts, looking gloomily down into the arbutus grove and hoped our talk hadn't upset Lorenzo. Then round the pine-trees he came, as cheerful as could be.

'Here's your coat. You'd left it on a rosemary bush and the dew will soon be heavy. I've put on a kettle for tea. The others will need it after their bathe.'

That evening at dinner he was happier.

'Think of it. I've made eight hundred pounds out of *Lady Chatterley*. I've never had so much money before all at once. What shall we do? I think we'll take a villa in Taormina. Yes, we'll take a villa and live like gentleman and have a butler. Do you remember, Frieda, when the Bs'[5] parlourmaid slipped and fell down the stairs to that huge dining-room and the plates crashed like a thunderstorm?'

'Yes, and Ada pretended it hadn't happened. So calm. She never even looked round but just went on talking.'

'That was awful,' Lorenzo said, giving the table a bang, 'it wasn't human. There we were, simply shattered, and that poor girl might have been badly hurt, but no, she must be a Buddha and sit there, far removed from mundane things—under a Bo-tree indeed!'

'Then do you remember how frightened they were in Ceylon? How the natives didn't like them being so holy?'

'What was that hymn Robert was always singing?' Throwing back his head Lorenzo chanted in a horrible falsetto:

> Oh to be nothing, nothing
> Oh to be nothing, *nothing*

and put diabolic yearning into it, repeating it again.

'Stop, please stop!' Richard almost shouted. Lorenzo gravely and politely stopped, the rapt theosophist to the end.

'There was an *amah* who tried to frighten them about snakes.'

'It was spiders, Frieda. Yes. The nights were black, oh black. The jungle was just outside the bungalow and it seemed to step closer and bend over us when the darkness came. Sounds boomed, and some animal shot a cry at you. Oooooouh or crrrcquck—like that. And this woman used to slip behind Ada and whisper "Lady sleep here, *this* room tonight. *Spider* in lady's bed and if spider bite *lady*, lady die".'

He drew out the dying into a long sigh. It would be dreadful if this gave the impression of vulgar, unkind mockery. No, apart from his intolerance of poses, Lawrence liked to present each actor to us so that we realised them. It pleased him to give us laughter, to hold us amused and wanting no other entertainment.

After coffee, when we were in the sitting-room, his mood changed. Press cuttings of *Lady Chatterley's Lover* had come and most of them were disgraceful. The critics had become so heated over imagined dirt that the odour of their sanctity was tainted. We were amused by these notices, forgetting that the author of the book was being hurt.

'My God!' one of us gave a shout. 'Here, in this one, Lorenzo, one of them calls you a cesspool!'

He made a grimace which might have been a smile or slight nausea.

'Really? One's fellow creatures are too generous. It's *quite* worth while giving of one's best, isn't it?' Then as if speaking to himself, Nobody *likes* being called a cesspool.'

Beside the fire there was a heap of light branches, rosemary, thorn and myrtle. They were used to kindle dying embers, but a devil suddenly came into Lawrence and he threw a branch on the flames. It crackled beautifully and he threw another and another. Fire filled the whole hearth-place, licking over the edges.

'What are you *doing*,' cried Frieda.

He didn't answer but two more branches went into the flames.

'Look out! It'd be a cold night in the open if you burnt us out.'

No answer, but quicker, more branches, more thorns. Painful smoke and lovely perfume began to fill the room. But each protest only made him add more fuel in a sort of rhythmical rage. His fury died out with the swiftly burnt herbs, and having served up his enemies symbolically as a burnt sacrifice, he never bothered about them again.

NOTES

For a note on Brigit Patmore see p. 145.

1. Lawrence's translation was published in Florence in 1929, with an introduction by Lawrence.

2. Giuseppe Orioli, Italian publisher and bookseller, published the first edition of Lawrence's *Apocalypse* in Florence in 1931.

3. Short story by Lawrence, first published in London in 1928 and later collected in the posthumous volume *Lovely Lady*.

4. Play by Lawrence published in 1926.

5. Presumably the Brewsters (see p. 159); 'Ada' in the next speech must be an error for 'Achsah'.

Lawrence in Bandol*

BREWSTER GHISELIN

One afternoon early in January 1929, while walking toward the railway station on the slopes above Bandol, I heard quick steps of approach and,

* *London Magazine*, v (Dec 1958) pp. 13–22.

looking up from the red earth of the roadside, saw a blonde woman and a red-bearded man in a faded sky-blue jacket striding rapidly towards me. The man was slender and slightly stooped, lithe and easy in motion. There was a country looseness in his figure and clothing. As they passed, I caught the glance of his clear blue eyes, and I thought, though the photographs had suggested dark hair and beard, this may be Lawrence.

In Paris I had written asking permission to come and see him. Expecting some days of waiting for his consent, that I never doubted would come, I had gone on at leisure to the south. His reply, already long delayed, must arrive within a day, and until then it would be better to say nothing.

A day or two later, on Friday, 4 January, I concluded that one of our letters must have miscarried and that if I was to see Lawrence at all before leaving for Nice the next Monday I had better try to find him. That afternoon, at the town hall I obtained his address. The Hôtel Beau-Rivage stood on a wooded rise along the western sweep of the shore, overlooking the harbour. On the gravel terrace before the hotel entrance, I paused to look down on the water and the plage. There, sitting alone and motionless on a bench against a small tree, was the man I had seen on the hill. He wore an overcoat and hat, and as if cold he was huddled a little, his head slightly forward and sideways in an attitude I afterwards knew to be characteristic.

Descending the long stone stairway, I crossed toward the water's edge and as he glanced up I asked, 'Are you Mr D. H. Lawrence? I'm the young American who wrote to you.' I explained how I had waited for his answer that had never come. 'Your letter or mine must have miscarried. I wouldn't have bothered you with such intrusion, except that I've needed to talk with you.'

Lawrence looked at me closely and asked me to sit down. He questioned me about what I was doing, how long I was staying, where I was going. I told him I had come to Europe mainly in the hope of seeing him, partly to find a graduate school in which the whole need of the mind would be of foremost concern, in order that my education might be an organic development of power rather than only a professional discipline. But during my first term as a graduate student at Oxford I had found much the same procedures, atmosphere, and expectations as at the universities in America. I said I was trying to find a fresh mode of life, a new way of being alive, that I had only intimations of, amid the stale ways of thought and feeling the world was content with. I said I believed he had gone far in discovering some such way of being and in developing a true understanding, that everyone else seemed to lack.

To most of this he answered briefly, or merely 'Yes...Yes,' in varying intonations of sympathy or acquiescence. Presently Mrs Lawrence came down the stairs from the hotel with a handsome young woman, her daughter Barbara Weekley, and I was introduced. We strolled along the sunny quay, toward the few moored pleasure boats and, beyond them, the many fishing boats scattered over the water. When the two women went on into town, Lawrence and I sat on a bench facing the sea.

There for more than an hour, under the palms in sunshine among the passing people, we talked of many things, of the intent and fate of his latest book, *Lady Chatterley's Lover*, which I had just read, of the plight of the civilised world, of England and America, and chiefly of means of keeping a vital awareness in our civilisation which was tending always to destroy it. Having read a dozen volumes of Lawrence, I was familiar with his terms of expression and with the outlines of his thought. He spoke casually and freely, with much variety of tone and feeling, often with humour, sometimes scornfully, never with solemnity. The value of his conversation lay less in the force of what was being said, for all its swift flexibility, diversity, colour, good sense, and constancy to a single vision of truth, than in the interest and charm of his presence, that this talk made articulate. I listened a great deal and asked a few questions.

The few words of *Lady Chatterley's Lover* which he had brought back into clean usage after their three hundred years on the dung-hill had lost him many of his following, he said. The old maids, as he called them with acid amusement, faithful until then, had shut the book with a snap. And yet those words were in good use, he declared, for fourteen hundred years; then 'the dirt of the Renaissance got on them'. His use of them was part of his effort to restore the confused, degenerated feelings of modern people. 'Sex,' he said, 'must be taken out of the WC.' There was no hope of a sane society otherwise.

'The uttermost mystery' for him, Lawrence said, was how man, in the state of an animal moving in instinctive unconsciousness, in dynamic relation with his environment, 'came to say "I am I"'. Now the whole world was 'under a net of ideas', and one must make holes in the net as a means of slipping through—and keep them open for others. If America should ever achieve a new way of life it could be only in the far future, for the psyche of all Americans was essentially European: 'Look how they take up one idea after another, while their feeling is the same old dead one!'

Still, he might be at his ranch in New Mexico in the summer, he conceded, and if he were I must come and visit him there. Even if he were not, I should go to the ranch and live there as long as I liked: a man could live in that country for a thousand dollars a year—for less on the ranch. I should see something of the Pueblo Indians, and if possible go into Mexico, learn something of the Aztec and Mayan civilisations, from which he himself had learned much.

Asked about England, he said he was always miserable there: the climate, but worst of all the hopelessness of the English. The working classes were alive when he was a boy, he said, and he would go back if he thought he could waken them; but he had not gone back; and he said he would not think or talk about it. 'I want to believe they aren't quite dead,' he finished. But while he spoke it was plain, from the misery of his voice and eyes, that he was sure they were.

The depression of his spirit was momentary, however. Lawrence was never doleful, he could not stand lugubriousness. In disgust, he ridiculed Keats's yearning for death and quoted with scorn, '"Now more than ever seems it rich to die"!'

By this time Mrs Lawrence had returned to sit with us. 'Do you like being here in Europe?' she asked.

Some things I had liked: at Oxford, a series of lectures on Greek vases, for instance; the sombre glass in the Cathedral at Chartres in the dusk, the hills and sea at Bandol. Finally I emphasised my distaste for the feeling in the cities and towns by a gesture toward the group of buildings behind us.

Lawrence, who had been musing and as if half listening, turned suddenly full around and urgently said, 'What is *wrong* with it? *What is wrong with it?*'

I answered, 'It's the people, it's the way of their being.' And indicating the facades along the water-front, I said I supposed everything a man laid his hand to took the impress of his being and gave it forth again.

He relaxed from the attitude into which he had moved with the energy of his question, and in a voice full of weariness, but alive with profound emotion that I can attribute only to humour, he said. 'Yes, yes, it's dead. Everything they touch is dead. Even if they make a little cake! Their bread—haven't you noticed it?—tastes of death.'

It was tea time, then, and they invited me to the hotel for tea, but I excused myself, suspecting they must be weary of me. Lawrence insisted that I come to lunch on the following day.

At noon next day they were waiting in the sunlight on the terrace before the hotel, and we went in immediately, to a white table at the north wall of the dining room. The soft-eyed young Negro who waited on us came from French Africa, they explained. As he stepped slowly, negligently about on his errands, Mrs Lawrence exclaimed with pleasure, 'He walks like Lorenzo!' And amid laughter Lawrence sat chuckling his appreciation and shaking his head in denial.

The talk went on in gaiety and extravagance. With humorous relish and some irony, Lawrence described a 'tea' in Hollywood, at which an appalling pint of whisky and soda was thrust into his hand by the host, an actor wearing white riding breeches and carrying a riding crop, while the shrinking refined wife drooped in a corner and a small son marched about dressed up exactly like father and swinging his little whip. Often Lawrence spoke vividly and unsparingly of human absurdity, but never coldly, never really uncharitably. He was without a trace of the delusions that drive so many to find their own elevation in the abasement of others.

After coffee on the terrace, we went upstairs to the Lawrences' rooms, on the second floor of the hotel overlooking the bay. Lawrence read aloud some of the *Pansies*[1] and the first 'Introduction', which he had recently completed. Finishing the passage on Swift's poem to Celia, he looked up in concern for whatever embarrassment his stepdaughter might be suffering. 'Poor Barby! *Poor* Barby!' he said, in caressing tones of sympathy tinged with amusement much as one might comfort a rain-soaked kitten, and went on with the reading.

That afternoon he showed me some of his paintings: *Leda*, and a watercolour of two figures in grey, terra cotta, and rose, and others. He had turned to painting, he said, as a means of defining some things better expressed in that way than in writing.

At the end of my visit, I spoke of leaving Bandol on the following Monday, to travel along the coast toward Italy, perhaps as far as Genoa, then back to Oxford to begin the new term. Lawrence said, 'Oxford is squalid!' and gave his opinion that I would have done better to live here and there in Europe instead of studying at Oxford.

The following morning the sky was grey over a level sea, the mimosas drooped with moisture, and the stems of the olives on the darkened hills were black with rain. The Lawrences were coming to tea at the hotel where I was staying, some distance along the road toward Toulon, quite outside the village. Though I was distressed to think they would need to come through ugly weather to see me, I could think of nothing appropriate to do, and at last did nothing. They arrived during a downpour, in a lumbering old taxi, but cheerful and friendly and full of reassurances that nothing was amiss. During the hour of their visit, Lawrence asked if I really wanted to travel on to Nice and other crowded places. When I admitted that I had no great interest in the journey, he suggested that I stay through my whole vacation in Bandol and that I come to the Beau-Rivage in order to be near them; he would arrange for me to have the choice of two vacant rooms across the hall from his own.

It was an invitation, I discovered, to become virtually a member of the Lawrence household. I was expected to share their activities through the day, to be with them in the evening, and to have a part in whatever plans were made. Breakfast, of course, in the Continental style, did not bring us together. After lunch in the dining room and coffee on the terrace, we spent the hours until tea time in talk and in walking along the shore. Every evening after dinner, we gathered in Mrs Lawrence's bedroom, Lawrence usually sitting on the bed, Barbara Weekley or I beside him, and Mrs Lawrence in a chair by the window. Often Lawrence read briefly from the manuscript he had written during the day, and I frequently carried some of it off later to my room. In this way I read his 'Introduction' to the *Paintings*[2] as it came from his pen and some of the *Pansies*.

Lawrence worked in the mornings, sitting in bed in his narrow room, facing the window and the sea, which usually was blue and white with sunshine. When I left my room after breakfast, his door was always shut, in the long, still, shadowy hall.

Until eleven o'clock or noon I was alone on the populous *plage*, sometimes writing or sketching. Then the Lawrences, with Barbara Weekley during the first five days, came down from the hotel to sit in the sun, to walk about, or to visit the teeming market in the square behind the church, to look on or to buy fruit.

In those days Bandol was little more than a lively village. Dogs foraged along the shore or haunted the market place, standing or lying in the luxury of human presence, among the booths, the racks of clothing, the live catch heaped in wet baskets or dropped on bare concrete. Women passed back and forth on their errands or in idleness, many of them wearing their fashionable bright red, purple, green, or black bed slippers. Fishermen in blue jeans sat against the railing around the war monument, talking and laughing while they mended their nets or baited their lines with small prawns and wound them into a basket like a nest, the hooks plunged in along the rims. Drying nets like a gross brown lace striped the quay. Lawrence liked the warm scene, the contentment of the men and their pleasure at their work.

One morning early in the week Lawrence came from the market to sit beside me, his pockets bagging full of yellow apples. The weather had warmed, after the snow and rain of the weekend, and the sea towards which we looked was a slick of light and the sky was a bright distance. Eating one of my large sweet tangerines, he said with musing pleasure, 'It tastes like Africa.' Less by his words than by the full texture of circumstance and scene, I knew his feeling and meaning. I recalled that during our first conversation he had spoken of his belief that the civilisations of the future would be in the sunny lands. It was not only for his health's sake, as some have said and continue to say, that Lawrence moved about the world. He went in search of light and to explore the various life in warm places and to enjoy it.

Bandol is in southernmost France. The winters are mild and sunny, and during most of that second week in January there was scarcely a cloud. Along the *plage* the broad palms flourished unpinched, and white circlets of flowers hung among the higher leaves of eucalyptus trees. Yet Lawrence was not wholly satisfied.

One afternoon we climbed the hills above Bandol, past fields of yellow and white narcissus, and up among the olives where the stones of centuries were piled between the trees, broad walls the height of a man, and further along paths among heather, where Lawrence pointed out to me wild rue and fumitory, and still higher past the pines. On the rocky ridge, Lawrence stood musing the ancient aspect of the land and talking of the races that had possessed it before the present. We looked down on a long inland valley, on many grey rocks, wild ridges blotched with pines, and further downslope the black cypresses, the fields, the olives and the deciduous trees about the few buildings.

'It's not far enough south,' he said.

Coming down from the ridge, Lawrence pondered his future. Though his publishers were eager for him to write another novel, he did not want to; he would not do it. 'If there weren't so many lies in the world,' he said, looking at me earnestly, 'I wouldn't write at all.' What he might do and where he would go remained uncertain. Many times, he said, he had felt it would take ever so little to make him an American, though not in the way of consciousness dominant in the United States, based on money, the universal disease of mental obsession. All the real America, he declared, moves in that 'deep, terrible, tigerlike vibration of destruction'—the opposite of Europe—which the aboriginal civilisations, Mayan, Aztec, Incan, and the dying civilisation of the Pueblos, realised so profoundly. Somebody should study the living remnant and 'find out where the Indians' energy comes from'. Even now, he felt, he might end in America, perhaps in the American way of being.

Lawrence meanwhile awaited without impatience what might define itself in him. He found satisfaction in what the place and time afforded, especially in human relationships, imperfect though these might be. He rarely preferred to be alone, and when he did, as one evening when he put on his overcoat and went out to walk in the dark, without inviting companions, he was not long away.

Lawrence responded to everything with the organic strength of his feeling for the substance and shape of life, in himself and around him. He was never indifferent. Yet sometimes he was quiet, or even quiescent, as on the blue and yellow afternoon of 9 January, when we walked out to the end of the jetty and sat on huge blocks of stone, dangling our legs over water. P. R. Stephensen,[3] the publisher, who had come to see Lawrence on business, was with us. The sun was warm, the wind light, and I wanted to swim, but my suit was far back at the hotel. Standing on cold slabs in the shadow in a deep slot between the blocks of stone, I made a loin cloth of two big coloured handkerchiefs, with one of Lawrence's for a belt. When I went into the breathless water over weed-darkened boulders, Lawrence nodded down to me from the rock against the sky, reassuring me: 'You're perfectly decent; you're perfectly decent,' he called. After some minutes I clambered on stones by the rockwall and stood in the ripple while Stephensen read aloud a story he had recently written.

The self of most men is important enough to demand protection and various enhancements. For Lawrence, self seemed to have no interest. This detachment was the source of some of his freedom. It perhaps accounts for his enormous, uncalculated generosity of spirit. He never withheld himself. He was unreflectingly bounteous, in kindness and sometimes, very rarely, in anger.

His anger is famous for the fury of its open outbursts, yet in all those days I saw him angry only once, in a flare of ferocity as he turned to Mrs Lawrence with a rebuke for her launching on a thoroughly Laurentian denunciation of some aspect of the world. 'You don't know anything about it!' he cried. Startled to stillness, she stared at him, her blue eyes glinting like rinsed china and her face tense and flushed. Almost at once it was over: he relaxed and turned to me quietly, smiling a little, with a brief comment on the evil of unfounded talk. Others could not change quite so abruptly, but within a few minutes the usual easy, lively atmosphere was restored.

On Thursday afternoon we took the bus to Toulon and there walked by the harbour and drank rum and coffee at a table before a café by the water. We wandered in the dark streets, bought roasted chestnuts, and looked over racks of flowers offered for sale. Afterwards we had tea in a quiet place. Waiting for Mrs Lawrence and Barbara Weekley, who had gone shopping, Lawrence and I talked of the disruptive and constructive effects of the presence of so many people intent on hasty routines.

Perhaps as a consequence of this feeling about the city, we chose on the following day, 11 January, to ride out on the sea in a motorboat instead of driving in a carriage inland to one of the hill towns, an alternative we had considered. The trip was planned for the afternoon.

Late in the sunny morning, Lawrence found me on the *plage* finishing a watercolour of some brilliant fingerlings I had bought in the market. He remarked on their vividness and on the full detail of the painting, for which he himself could never have found enough patience, he said. If I should do a series of such paintings, he suggested, they could probably be exhibited at Dorothy Warren's[4] gallery in London. Yet one should work only when one wanted to, he warned me; it was wonderful how ability grew if one did that.

Most of all he was concerned about the uncoloured ground of white around the figures. He felt the paper—yet in all watercolour he worked with he felt 'the tyranny of the paper'. The feeling for the fishes themselves was true, he said, but they were isolated in the midst of bare space in a way that deprived them of their actual relation to other things, to water, for instance. My pleasure in setting them apart like intense flames in consciousness was 'a form of spiritual will desiring power', refusing to admit and to express the relatedness, the vital interchange, between them and all other things, each in their special quality and degree.

'I think the consciousness of the future will be intuitive,' Lawrence said, 'in its intellectual form a knowledge of relations.'

Early that afternoon, in an open motor boat, we travelled out on the sea to circle some lonely islands. All but one of them, on which the lighthouse stood, were desolate stones stuck up into the midst of sun and sea. As we passed over pale green streaks in the deep channels Lawrence remarked that the colour was of sunken limestone, but the boatman confirmed my belief, based on knowledge of similar waters and seaground in California, that it was the pallor of sand. Passing one of the smaller islands, a sunny slab over a cold shadow of waves, I remarked that I would like to go onto it.

'*Why?*' Lawrence asked sharply, as if scenting folly.

'Just to be there,' I answered.

'Yes,' he conceded after an interval, as if he had been considering.

Beyond the familiar hills of the shore other hills had lifted into view, the inland upland rising snowless toward the white bar of the farthest mountains. We must have been four or five miles from land when Lawrence told the boatman to turn round. The ride back was colder.

It was probably that same afternoon that we went downshore past the town to a little tea garden under pepper and eucalyptus trees by the sea. The sun would be down in an hour. Though the air was beginning to chill, I intended to go swimming again; I had brought a suit and towel this time. But Lawrence fiercely forbade it, because of the increasing cold, and in order not to distress him I gave up and sat still with the others, talking and drinking hot coffee.

We used to go a good deal along that eastward stretch of shore. One of our pleasures was seeing a flock of about forty goats that often grazed near the roadside, attended by a fat man. Idly watching his flock, he would sit like a slightly deflated balloon, while beside him his dwindled black dog lay breathing with closed eyes and pricked ears. The man's faintest whistle would make the goats swerve like a pool of minnows. When we whistled, the goats heard nothing.

On my last afternoon in Bandol, Tuesday, 15 January, Lawrence and I walked together along the shore a mile or so eastward toward Toulon. Near the mouth of a little creek we sprawled on the gravel beside the waves to talk. 'A flower is the most perfect expression of life,' Lawrence said. He liked the symbol of the Lotus, 'coming out of the mud'. What was wrong with all the religions was that they had always 'plucked the lily', had found one or another symbol and had clung to it, refusing to relinquish it as its vitality was exhausted. Yet a symbol, he had found, lasted only about twenty minutes—he didn't know why; then it had to be replaced by another. The ultimate symbol he called 'the Sun, the great central sun around which all the universe are circling'. Sometimes he preferred, he said, the symbol of the great white bird beating the water with its wings and sending out waves. I asked why he did not write a book about symbols, and he answered slowly, as if reflecting, that he might, sometime.

I looked at him without speaking, feeling that though I had understood in some degree I could not wholly reach him. Coming down the shore, we had talked of the difficulty of conveying new insight, of the likelihood that even the clearest embodiment of it will be misunderstood, as so much of his work had been, and of the fact that apprehension of any new work of art requires a growth of consciousness, an expansion of the psyche, in the perceiver. I knew that insight is a living thing and that in full understanding of Lawrence's work I must comprehend in myself a vast fabric of living experience.

Knowing he would interpret my words by their context and sense their irony, I said, 'Even I don't really understand you.'

'No,' he said soberly, 'no...'

Early next morning when I was ready for the train, I went to the Lawrences' rooms to say goodbye. In the clear full light before sunrise Lawrence sat in bed, propped against the headboard. We said only a few words and shook hands. His eyes were on mine while I crossed to the door at the foot of his bed and went out.

NOTES

Brewster Ghiselin (born 1903), American scholar and teacher, latterly Professor of English at the University of Utah. His recollections of a visit to Lawrence in January 1929 were published almost thirty years later. Bandol is on the south coast of France between Toulon and Marseilles; the Lawrences arrived there on 17 November 1928.

1. Volume of poems by Lawrence published in July 1929 by Secker of London in bowdlerised form, fourteen poems of the original collection being omitted. The latter were not published in England or the USA until 1964. See also n. 2 below.

2. Privately printed in 1929. The manuscript (and also that of *Pansies*: see n. 1 above) was seized in the post on the instructions of the Home Secretary, Sir William Joynson-Hicks. Questions were asked in the House of Commons concerning this incident (see Moore, pp. 396–9).

3. A publisher, editor and author who published an unexpurgated edition of *Pansies* in Paris in August 1929.

4. Dorothy Warren, a niece of Lady Ottoline Morrell, exhibited Lawrence's paintings at her gallery in Maddox Street, London, in the summer of 1929.

Lawrence in Bandol: Another Account*

RHYS DAVIES

I went in trepidation. The visit was important to me. Just as his books had meant as much to me as all my own experiences of life, becoming mixed with those experiences, I thought this meeting would intensify what he had already given me. For the younger generation of writers in England then, in that strange confused directionless decade after the war, he alone seemed to be carrying a torch. True, a smoky, wild torch. But nevertheless a light, though exactly on what path it was shedding illumination was often a matter for dispute, quarrel and even derision. I think we admired him because he was not sitting down inertly during those slack years. He was

* From 'D. H. Lawrence in Bandol', *Horizon*, II (Oct 1940) pp. 191–201, 202–3.

crying aloud, if sometimes incoherently, of the deceit, falseness and dangers of those apparently victorious after-war years. Not that he was political, or even social, minded. His message was directed into the heart, the loins and what he would call 'the bowels of mankind'. Meaning instinct as opposed to the mechanisation of the individual. His work was a fresh announcement of life. Furthermore, he used language as no one had used it before.

In the train I asked myself what I thought he'd be like as a person—he had written to say he would meet me at the station, and I had seen only one photograph of him, a youthful one. I found I thought of him as a big sombre man with a vehement beard, traces of his mining *milieu* in him, rugged, savage and a little rude. Yet though he was not big, sombre or unkempt, as I descended from the train I instantly recognised him in the crowd on the platform—and he me—and there he was smiling, even gay, his high voice rippling and easy as he asked me about the journey. Standing on a rock at the gateway of the station, Mrs Lawrence, aloft, handsome and bright-plumaged, was searching over the heads of the people for us. She, too, was gay and cheerful. It seemed something happy, even a joke, that I had come safely the short distance from Nice. In the car we chattered like magpies. My nervous excitement and twinges of fear fled. I was very glad I had come. Lawrence looked at me keenly with his bright, perhaps too bright, eyes and smiled; Frieda laughed, and I felt livelier than I had done for a long time. Just then I did not feel I had approached the wilderness habitation of one who, feeding on locusts and wild honey, was lifting his terrible voice against the world.

This first note of frivolous gaiety, alas, was not always to be maintained. I, like everybody who came into contact with him, got my share of St John the Baptist denunciation. But for that first hour or two all was charm and ease. We entered the drowsy, placidly-run hotel purring at each other: it was the hotel to which Katherine Mansfield used to bring her nervous exhaustion and her lady-Hamlet diary. There was an air of tranquil indolence. The milky blue sea was lazy under the hotel windows.

Lawrence was a small thin man with a most fascinating head. Finely shaped, his head had both delicacy and rude strength. His beard and hair, of a ruddy brown, shone richly and, with his dark eyes, were keen with vitality. His hands were sensitively fine, and beautiful in movement. These features suggested a delicacy that at last had been finely tempered from ages of male and plebeian strength: a flower had arrived from good coarse earth. His thinness was neat, lively, and vibrant with awareness of others. To be with him was to feel a different and swifter beat within oneself. The stupid little behaviour of ordinary life, the little falsehoods, the little attitudes, rituals and poses, dropped away and one sat with him clear and truthful.

That first evening I spoke, when alone with Mrs Lawrence, of the admiration and respect of the *young* people in London, how eagerly we looked to Lawrence, how mocking we were of the officious pomposities of the enthroned gods. 'You must tell him that,' she said quickly, 'it will please him so much. Because he feels they *all* hate him.' I told Lawrence, as sincerely as I could. But he was doubtful. I insisted. He shook his head unbelievingly. I became perplexed: didn't the man *want* admiration and disciples, I asked myself a little angrily and unable to see, just then, that he had been so wounded by English attacks that his old cry of anguish, 'They are all against me', had become at last a blindly violent mania.

Thereupon Lawrence broke into such abuse of the young that I was discomfited. Ah, why didn't they stand up, he fumed, and fight to make the world theirs, why didn't they smash, smash, smash? Why did they tolerate the impositions of the old world, the old taboos and the mongrel trashy contacts of the civilisation they were forced into? The men did not know even how to handle a woman: they wanted to be treated as women themselves: and the women were lost, senseless, vicious—but because their men had failed them.

Yet his arraignment of the young was not so wholehearted as his fierce raging hatred of the generation that sat in tight yet flabby ruling of the world, the moneyed and the governing classes particularly. It was they who were rotting the world, it was they who closed themselves to the voice of the spirit and lived only in the vulgar transaction of being worldlily successful, of attaining at all costs the power to grind down someone else. The young he blamed for allowing them to do it without protest.

'Kick,' he said, 'kick all the time, make them feel you know what they are. Because you *do* know, you're intelligent enough. The young know, they *know*, and yet they let be. Oh dear, it drives me to despair when I see them holding back, letting be. Because your chance is now; the world is all wobbling and wants a new direction.'

And his voice, become shrill as he was roused—and how easily he was roused to an extreme pitch of intensity!—would finish in a heave of sighing despair. Later he spoke of the way those elders had tried to curb him, how, indeed, they *had* curbed him. 'I know I'm in a cage,' he rapped out, 'I know I'm like a monkey in a cage. But if anyone puts a finger in my cage, I bite—and bite hard.'

Uneasy though such tirades as these made me, I saw then that he was certainly caged. He was caged by censorship and persecution chiefly, but there was also his consumption and the exile this meant; and he was caged by the contempt, the laughter, the cheap sneers and the suggestive and cunning propaganda of his enemies who spoke and wrote of him at that time (*Lady Chatterley's Lover*[1] had not long been published) as a frustrated sexual maniac, pornographic and indecent. Caged, which was the same thing as a retreat to the desert, he had arrived at that prophetic stage (and these were the last two years of his life) when the civilised human race appears one day as effete idiots, another as a pack of hyenas and wolves.

But, though he writhed away, he could not turn his back on people, he could not rid himself of his vehement awareness of people: this was the motive power of his tremendous nervous vitality—and this it was that was treacherously exhausting his body. His condition at this period might have been called tragic. Yet, because of that passionate awareness still burning in him, one could not think of him as anything but a great dynamo of life, still generating with a wealthy fertility the magic of existence. Those pungent, energetic and fecund recent books of his!

At this time in Bandol he was writing the satirical poems to be called *Pansies* and also painting one or two pictures. He told me he would write no more novels; *Lady Chatterley's Lover* was to be his last long work of fiction, the last large attempt to tell men and women how to live. For all his fury and rages, he got immense fun out of writing *Pansies*. He would write them in bed in the mornings, cheerful and chirpy, the meek sea air blowing in from the enchanting little bay outside his window. He sat up in bed, a little African straw cap on the back of his head—'It keeps my brain warm,' he said, afterwards presenting me with another of these little native caps. There was something perky and bird-like about him thus, and he was intensely happy and proud of the *Pansies*; he would read out the newest ones with delight, accentuating the wicked sharp little pecks in them. He little thought of the ridiculous heavy-handed official interference these vivid little lizards of poems were about to endure.[2] Yet in the end they emerged triumphant, with their tails gaily up.

But it was out of his painting he seemed to get the most joy, turning to it with relief and a sense of escape that perhaps in words was denied him—for in all Lawrence's later books, luxuriant though they are with vivid life, there is an unhappy sense of recoil, as if the full blaze of his soul could not be got entirely on the pages and the writer had retired baffled into himself again, to brood and gather strength for another terrific outrush. But on a canvas he could paint those rich sensuous shades he loved so much, paint them in their own colours, not in black words; he could give a goat or a swan actual shape, a tree, a flower, a nude, in their own colours. Yet, being Lawrence and not a novelist playing about with paint, it was not enough to give them pictorial representation; there must be that exuberant surge of passion, so that every line and every shade of those nudes, flowers and animals must blaze with it. At their London exhibition (which was raided by the police) the pictures embarrassed people, the Lawrence vehemence was too naked on canvas, it confronted one too suddenly. A book is more secretive, its appeal slower: particularly the Lawrence books have to be read several times before they yield their full meaning. It was said the paintings were faulty in drawing and construction, bad *pictures*—as undoubtedly they were. But because of that Lawrence intensity in them the technical errors seemed not to matter; almost because of the errors they achieved a barbaric aliveness. And to their painter they gave intense joy, they were so actual before his eyes, giving visual representation to a sensuousness he tried to get into words. He was almost pathetic in his absorption in these paintings; he said that words bored him now.

> . . . my soul is burning
> as it feels the slimy taint
> of all those nasty police-eyes like snail-tracks smearing
> the gentle souls that figure in the paint . . . [3]

he wrote after the police-raid in London. The opinion, sometimes expressed even now, that Lawrence sought deliberately to incur official censorship, is completely false. I was with him often during the police and newspaper activities over *Lady Chatterley* and *Pansies*. Their effect on him was either like a spiritual vomiting or a fury that made his very appearance that of a demon. And he had not the kind of calculation to scheme all this out. Of the many accusations made against him nothing could be more fantastically untrue than that he was a humbug.

Once he rapped out at me: 'All you young writers have me to thank for what freedom you enjoy, even as things are, for being able to say much that you couldn't even hint at before I appeared. It was I who set about smashing down the barriers.'

The afternoons and evenings were given over to idleness. Walking tired him, so he would dawdle at the edge of the sea in the sun. These afternoons in the sun with him seemed to have a living peace that was strangely refreshing; he seemed to spread around him, his rages quietened for a while, a conciliatory atmosphere of awareness, so that the lazy roll of the sea, that ancient and ever-young blue sea, and the voices of the naked boys at play on the *plage* (it was his picture of these boys that was the chief cause of the London raid), became a harmony that gave, to me at least, a fresh and satisfying ease. He would ask me about my childhood in Wales, my home life, my reactions to the constrictions and religious bigotry of a nonconformist period. He said:

What the Celts have to learn and cherish in themselves is that sense of mysterious magic that is born with them, the sense of mystery, the dark magic that comes with the night especially, when the moon is due, so that they start and quiver, seeing her rise over their hills, and get her magic into their blood. They want to keep that sense of the magic mystery of the world, a moony magic. That will shove all their nonconformity out of them.

Another time he broke into a lamentation for the old pre-war England, shaking his bearded head, his voice becoming hollow with the realisation that that England was dead: 'Ah, you young don't know what England could mean. It's all been broken up for you, disrupted. I'm glad I was born at my time. It's the sense of adventure that's gone, and there wasn't all this ashy taste in the mouth. The fun is gone. That's what you haven't got.'

And though he would speak with contempt and anger of the economic poverty of his childhood and the horrible dreariness that trails behind mining-village life, his days in those districts of his youth seemed, as he talked, to have given him intense glee and satisfaction. He would tell of some of the characters of Derbyshire,[4] so that bits of old England stood out before me with Shakespearean gusto.

'But nowadays,' he lamented, 'all pleasure takes place in people's heads. They don't *do* and *live* funny things any more, they've become much too mental and smart. The old England is gone and you've let her slip away.' Again and again he harped on the inertia of the young in not springing to save the real, beautiful England. And, because of his tuberculosis, one couldn't taunt him with his own long exile from the damp soggy land. Besides, was he not protesting enough in his books?

An interesting admission he made to me was that he had come to respect his father much more than when he wrote *Sons and Lovers*. He grieved having painted him in such a bitterly hostile way in that book. He could see now that his father had possessed a great deal of the old gay male spirit of England, pre-puritan, he was natural and unruined deep in himself. And Lawrence, by implication, criticised his mother who had so savagely absorbed him, the son. Frieda told me, in answer to my opinion that *Sons and Lovers* was Lawrence's finest book, 'No, it's an evil book, because of that woman in it, his mother.' I was, of course, judging the book as a literary creation.

Lawrence was exceedingly puritan himself in many things, and very chapel-English. He was even an old-maidish prude. One evening I repeated a coarsely funny story that was going the rounds of the Riviera just then. It was received in blank silence. No, not blank; a silence full of freezing reproach. Stories that pulled a face at sex and teased it he abhorred. On the other hand, one was allowed to use in ordinary conversation all the 'indecent' words, all those expressive words used by sailors, navvies and undergraduates which can so neatly abridge and clarify one's sentences. Which was a kind of concession.

Crotchety though he was at times, he seldom irritated me. He was so entirely without reserve, he was so aware of one, his personality came forth with such a full glow, sometimes in a martial march, true but most often in a bright recognition that had a sturdy, ardent eagerness. To argue with him was difficult. In spite of one's frequent mental doubt, elsewhere in one's being there was the feeling that, in some burning world beyond logic, he was supremely right. If one could cut away all the weeds of principles and behaviour that had got into one since self-consciousness began, one felt that there, in the natural, instinctive self, was the truth that lived in him so undiminished. He wrote in one of his studies: 'The soul has many motions, many gods come and go. Try and find your deepest issue, in every confusion, and abide by that. Obey the man in whom you recognise the Holy Ghost; command when your honour comes to command.' And I remember his saying to me: 'When you have come to a decision, whatever your mental calculations tell you, go by what you feel here'—and with his quick intent gesture he placed his hands over and around his belly—'go by that, what you feel deep in you, not by what your head tells you.'

He was obsessed by the mischief done by 'mentality' when it usurped the emotions or feeling or, perhaps, that Holy Ghost of which he wrote, the uncontaminated texture in a man which must be preserved if he is to live truly. Modern literature suffered from mentality almost completely, he complained. Cerebral poems, creations of witch-novelists, with characters 'like those wooden figures in a child's Noah's Ark'. Cerebral fornications made modern novels indecent. And he would give a broadly amusing burlesque of some of his very famous literary contemporaries, all 'gorping and puffing away importantly for success'.

He had a magical talent for burlesque, and his performance of a certain novelist as a pompous whale churning the literary seas and spouting up water was so realistic that both the great industrious novelist and the stupid mass of whale were present in the room, but miraculously united. In the same way he could evoke flowers, animals and reptiles out of the air with a wonderful cunning. Once he described the lively adventures of his Italian terrier with such marvellous absorption into the canine world that D. H. Lawrence disappeared and I, too, felt myself turning into a dog: I remember especially his acting of the dog's writhing agony after it had been run over, its will to live, its pleased sniffing at life as it recovered, and its sudden bouncing forward into a fresh world of smells. He was that dog. This power of entering the soul of non-human things is the characteristic I remember most clearly. In the same way, it is for his vital descriptions of landscape and 'spirit of place', and of flowers, beasts and trees, that his books yield one most *pleasure* now.

At the hotel was a young negro waiter. Lawrence took, in his usual energetic way, a deep dislike to the youth. The dislike was so intense and its object so innocently unaware of it that I was vastly amused. To see Lawrence's eyes gleam with watchful revulsion as the waiter laid a dish on the table seemed utterly grotesque to me: why be so stirred over the young man? It was his hands Lawrence watched: thin dusky nervous hands laying very, very carefully a plate of *vol-au-vent* on the table. I watched too, as I had been bade.

'You saw his hands, how uncertain they were, no feeling in them! No feeling. It's quite sickening, he can't even place a plate down properly, he fumbles, hesitates, it's like a dead hand moving, every moment I expect to see the dish go to the floor.' And the denunciation came, as I expected. 'All his movements are so *mental*, he doesn't trust to his blood, he's afraid. Look at him walking down the room now, look at his legs, look how they hang together and cower, pushed forward only by his mind. Ugh!' And he ended with a sharp hiss of absolute revulsion. It was true, as I looked carefully at the young man's legs, that they were rather soft and dejected-looking, clinging together as though for company as he took his short, gliding kind of step down the room. Yes, his gait was vaguely unpleasant, I decided, that hesitating glide, as though practised, and the legs with their subjected look. There was little that was spontaneous, certainly, about the youth. But this fierce antipathy!

Of course, out of such vehemence and such antipathy came *Lady Chatterley's Lover* and *Women in Love*, and the others.

Then there was the English maiden lady in the hotel, one of those respectable spinsters who were scattered all over the South of France and Italy. This lady, he swore, would have liked to kill him. Her social advances had been ignored. And one evening he wouldn't deliver up to her the hotel *Daily Mail* as she hovered and twittered about for it; he had whisked round to her demanding: 'Do you *want* this paper? I'm reading it.' The lady had shrunk back, mumbling that, no, she did not want the paper. But he had seen murder in her. In a shrill way he declared to me: 'She would have had me taken out and killed then and there.' The following morning—her bedroom was next to his—he insisted that through the dividing wall waves of hate and murder had been arriving from her. I think he saw her as some sort of witch. However, I was glad to see, on my next visit to Bandol, that he had made his peace with the lady. They now met on the common ground of painting. She made little water-colours of local scenes; Lawrence did his strident nudes. They almost flirted together with their brandished paint-brushes. Frieda was malicious. 'One of Lorenzo's old maids,' she said, telling me he had a weakness for these English spinsters.

Observing him strolling about in the sunshine of the *plage* below the hotel terrace, I mused over his extraordinary attraction as a person. In a faded old blue jacket, wispy trousers and a black flapping hat, he moved about with a springy awareness. There was something of both a bird and a lizard about him, light and winging, no flesh. Perky, bird or lizard like. Yet the thundering torrents, black hatreds and teeming awareness in that frail figure! Just then I felt, rather than was mentally aware of, the struggle against death-processes that was taking place in him. (I remembered he had just written a poem about a November sun—'my sun' sinking 'wintry but dauntless' into the west: was it prophetic?). The curiously fiery little figure winging about the *plage* was somehow electrically dangerous; it bore a high voltage of life. No, it could not die, with that bright eagerness in its wings.

His irascibility and irritation had the sharp, crackling, devouring temper of a fire. There was nothing small and fussy in his outbursts. They came in an avalanche, a torrent, a flood. Even over such a trivial incident as being half-an-hour late for the hotel lunch. I had met Frieda on the *plage* and we dawdled in a café over our apéritifs—time fled; it was enchanting to sit before that unspoilt (as it was then) native little *plage* of Bandol in the morning sun, while the villagers flopped about lazily in their carpet slippers. Unconscious that we were late we ambled back to the hotel. Suddenly I saw, watching our strolling approach from the top of the flight of steps leading to the hotel terrace, a dark sinister figure poised as if to swoop down on us, a malign vulture.

As we mounted the steps he was literally dancing with rage. What he said actually I don't remember, but as he hopped about, gesticulating in his Italian way, he poured out a flood of words that seemed to reduce the universe to nothing. He was the serpent come out of the heart of chaos to hiss forth death and desolation. I was interested, objectively, but decided that before such passion a polite apology for being late would be fatuous. And quite soon the tornado subsided into a vexed silence out of which came, presently, a charming offer. In the dining-room was a tray of newly-caught lobsters. These were a supplement on the table d'hôte price. Lawrence, the host, pointed them out and, coaxingly, was sure that I would like a lobster. I shook my head. He insisted. Then *I* became cantankerous. I refused to be wooed with lobsters. Frieda was not so silly. She enjoyed the fish with an unruffled air of 'however extraordinary my husband, one does not have lobsters every day'.

There were times when I could not bear to have him near me, and I would leave the hotel and go for long walks. It was the only way to keep one's will intact in this over-potent intimacy. He was too much of a magician, too much of an enchanter. There were times, indeed, when in everything he was too much. This, of course, was because I was still in a world which he had long ago left in disgust. I was even glad when it was time for me to leave Bandol, though for the next few months I returned again and again, glad to go to him, as I was glad to leave him. But such a dominant force as his was not for continual companionship. I do not wonder that his old cherished scheme for founding a community of fellow spirits came to nothing. For all his charm, aliveness and interest, men, unless they were completely negative, could never live for long in peace with Lawrence. And he had no use for negative people.

His marriage seemed to me a prosperous one. Frieda had a lioness quality that could meet his outbursts with a fine swing and dash: when really stung, she would shake her mane and grunt and growl; sometimes she charged. Their life together was an opulent one; her spirit was direct and generous, and his was laughing, malicious and subtle. Their notorious brawls were grand. She would lash out, and, gathering his forces with confident ease, he met her like a warrior. He would attack her for smoking too many cigarettes, having her hair cropped, taking a wrong line of thought, eating too many cakes in a café at Toulon, or for trying to be intellectual or aristocratic. He kept her simmering, subtly; for a natural inclination to a stout German placidity threatened to swamp her fine lioness quality.

*   *   *

Pansies was finished and typed in Bandol; an incomplete set was dispatched to England from that village post-office of tolerant France. We dawdled through the mild days, sometimes taking long drives into the country in the village droshky: Lawrence disliked motor-cars. Out in the country, while the ancient nag munched the herbage and Frieda and I strolled about, he would squat on his heels collier-fashion and remain thus for an hour, unmoving, haunched up like a very old and meditating bird, his shut eyelids lifted to the sun. There was something eternal and primitive about him thus; and a delicate, untrammelled peace. Sometimes he would open one eye like an owl, keep it briefly on me and Frieda, and lapse back into his meditation.

There was nothing of the cathedral air of the great writer about him; no pomp, no boomings, no expectation of a respectful hush from apprentice hands such as myself. One warm afternoon he announced, after a hint from me, that he would read a selection of *Pansies* to me and Frieda. After a rather heavy lunch we went to my bedroom, where there was a sofa, on which I foolishly lay. And Lawrence had not a good reading voice; it was apt to become stringy and hollow. Very soon, to the sound of verses about the harsh flight of swans clonking their way over a ruined world, I went off into deep slumber. When I woke he and Frieda had stolen away. But when we met at tea-time he twinkled with amusement. Only Frieda's face contained a surprised rebuke.

In a few days news came of the fussy official interference with *Pansies*, the opening and seizing of the packet of incomplete MSS in the post by the English authorities. It afterwards appeared that anything posted from Bandol to England just then was subject to scrutiny; it was known that the author of *Lady Chatterley* was living in the village. What a surprise the authorities must have had, really, for there was nothing in even the complete *Pansies* which could be described as indecent by a normal person. A few quips and bits of plain-speaking, in good household English; that was all. Still, they kept this incomplete collection. Afterwards I despatched from Nice another incomplete set, which arrived intact, and later I took to England a complete set, which was duly printed—though privately—and sold unexpurgated. Though I had no hand in the printing of this private edition, it was whispered to me one day on good authority that the flat in which I was staying had become of interest to the police: it was believed to be a distributing centre for the banned works of D. H. Lawrence. The fussiness!

Lawrence, sick in the face, crying out in his bedroom of the seizing of his darling, innocent poems, or raging on the beach as he talked of it, was depressing. He could *not* understand this new mealy-mouthed England. Ah, how the old robust England of strong guts and tongues had died! Why, why couldn't they let him have his say! The charge of indecency had an effect on him like vomiting. It was almost painful to look at him. It was in such moments as these that I felt that, more than his consumption, an evil destructive force was attacking him successfully.

NOTES

Rhys Davies, born 1903, is an Anglo-Welsh novelist and writer of short stories. Lawrence invited him to Bandol late in 1928.

1. Lawrence's novel was privately printed in Florence (1928) and Paris (1929); expurgated editions were published in London and New York in 1932. The earliest edition was vehemently attacked by some British newspapers: *John Bull* (20 Oct 1928), for instance, titled its article 'Famous Novelist's Shameful Book: A Landmark in Evil', described Lawrence as a 'bearded satyr', and spoke of the 'beastliness' of the book. This review is given in full in Nehls, III, pp. 262–5. For other reviews, see R. P. Draper (ed.), *D. H. Lawrence: The Critical Heritage* (London: Routledge & Kegan Paul, 1970). *Lady Chatterley's Lover* was banned but circulated widely underground in the ensuing years; the unexpurgated version became available in England only in 1960, and only then after an unsuccessful prosecution for obscenity (see p. 121).

2. See p. 262, nn. 1 and 2.

3. From the poem 'Give me a Sponge'.

4. Error for Nottinghamshire.

In Paris*

RHYS DAVIES

In Paris I witnessed another of his strange rages. We took a taxi to Sylvia Beach's book-shop in a little street near the Odeon; he wanted to ask Miss Beach if she would publish *Lady Chatterley*; she had already dared Joyce's *Ulysses* (a book Lawrence had not much respect for: too *cerebral*). The taxi-driver, a big bull-necked creature, couldn't find the little street. As we cruised for the second time round the Odeon, Lawrence began to start and writhe. The powerful, unmoving back of the driver roused him to a yell. 'The fat fool!' he screeched—in English—'A taxi-driver! Fool, fool, fool,'

---

* From *Horizon*, II (Oct 1940) pp. 204–7.

he stamped and writhed. 'Or else he's doing it purposely, knowing we are foreigners.' In the tiny enclosed space it was like having a shrill demented monkey beside me. After dipping into another street, again the cab cruised round the Odeon. To Lawrence's yells and bangs on the glass screen the driver's steady bull neck remained unperturbed. Ruddy beard stuck out, Lawrence's pale face was lifted in agony. The immovable neck in front was bringing on a psychic crisis.

At last the shop was discovered, and the taxi skipped up to the kerb softly as a purring cat. Lawrence's thin body exploded out of the door; I followed in readiness for a brawl on the pavement. But I was disappointed. The two men faced each other. The driver's big moony face was shining with a most childlike grin; it was all a friendly joke to him. And in heavy French he told us that he was a Russian, an exile, and had only recently begun his job as taxi-driver. He beamed with good humour; Russian-like, he accepted Lawrence's fury with benign understanding. Lawrence had started back from that broad Slav fleshy face. I could almost see the steam of his rage evaporating. His prancings became stilled. As we entered Miss Beach's shop he said to me, 'I *couldn't* be angry with him, I couldn't. Did you see his face! Beautiful and human. He lives in his blood, that man, he is solidly in his blood—not like these slippery French who are all mind. I saw it at once and I respected him.' Miss Beach was not interested in an edition of *Lady Chatterley*.

Though the weather was warm and sunny, and Paris at its best, he hated it, like all cities. He couldn't bear people close-packed about him, the grey slick city faces, and he would scuttle back to our hotel in Montparnasse after meals. We stayed there a month, and all the time he fumed to get away, the city darkened his spirit and humanity became almost completely hopeless. Knowledge of his presence got about, and he was offered a banquet by a literary organisation: to his horror. His chest became ominously troublesome. But such was the vitality he spread about him, even in Paris, that alarm and suspicion of his physical state would vanish.

It was in Paris that he dauntlessly refused to keep an appointment, made by a friend, with a first-class specialist in bronchial diseases. Half an hour before the time fixed, and ready dressed to go to the specialist, he suddenly refused to leave the hotel. It seemed to me that he believed a submission to medical art was an act of treachery to the power within him, his gods.

But his nights became restless; often I woke to his coughing and writhing in the next room. One night, instinctively, but half asleep, I hurried through the communicating door and found him as though in mortal combat with some terrible invisible opponent who had arrived in those mysterious dead hours that follow midnight. The dark tormented face and haggard body was like some stormy El Greco figure writhing on the bed. Was this the perky bird or lizard figure of Bandol! He seemed to be violently repudiating some evil force, a wretched man nearly overcome by a sinister power of superhuman advantages. Alarmed, I suggested a doctor and went towards the telephone. But at once he flew into anger. No, he would *not* have a doctor. But if I would sit quietly by the bed for a while... I think he needed the aid of some human presence. Soon he was calmer, lay back exhausted, unspeaking but triumphant. The opponent had gone.

A month passed before a publisher for *Lady Chatterley* was found.[2] Frieda returned from Germany; I left for England. My regret at leaving him was mingled with a strange willingness to go. He seemed to have given me as much as I wanted, and for me he would always be near. I have spoken to many people who did not know Lawrence personally but who read his books sympathetically, and to each of them he has been alive and of the same significance as though they sat with him and were warmed by that rich personal glow of his: and they too, like myself, when he died felt for a time as though there was no sun in the world. There must have been few men who inspired such personal—but I cannot find the word: not *affection*, not *homage*, *love* is too specialised a word, and I must say, almost meaninglessly—reactions, as Lawrence. Almost that emotion he inspired has been lost: to-day particularly we are consumed with distrust of the world and therefore men. Perhaps if that emotion had been garnered and understood and cherished, the life of man would have taken a more fruitful direction—for has the world ever been more sterile than it is now, except of wars? He was a Christ of an earthly estate, and those about him knew the Godhead he had found in himself, and were warmed by it. His humanity was so purely aristocratic and undefiled. Here was the complete flowering of the spirit in flesh. Let me not be misunderstood: Lawrence was a man and no Jesus in rapt love with the Heaven that is to come; but a Christ of himself as every man can become who has once found the pure centre of his being and keeps it uncontaminated. This is what he had done. He had not submitted to the contamination that seems inevitable. Civilisation had not dirtied him, in himself, though enough mud was thrown at him, and some clung for a space. It was the mud that caused those rages which seemed to be so insane.

He wrote to me now and again: gay, amusing letters, gay even in his furies against certain actions and persons in London. He wanted to start a little magazine, to be called *The Squib*, which was to consist of lampoons, leg-pulls and satiric pieces; he sent some verses for it and asked if I would be editor, with himself as guarantor of half the expenses. If he had lived it would have been a lively magazine, though I had a taste of how difficult it would have been to obtain suitable contributions; people jeered and lampooned amusingly enough in their conversations, but to get them to set their antipathies and violences on paper!—no, they became self-conscious and wary, the labour was impossible. The idea of *The Squib*, with Lawrence adopting the pseudonym of John Doolittle, came to nothing in the end.

NOTES

For a note on Rhys Davies, see p. 272.
1. Edward Titus published the novel in Paris in May 1929.

'An Inspired Provincial' *

NORMAN DOUGLAS

. . . the prevalent conception of Lawrence as a misanthrope is wrong. He was a man of naturally blithe disposition, full of childlike curiosity. The core of his mind was unsophisticated. He touched upon the common things of earth with tenderness and grace, like some butterfly poised over a flower—poised lightly, I mean, with fickle *insouciance* (for his books contain strange errors of observation).This, once more, was the direct reaction, the poet's reaction; the instantaneous record. No intervening medium, no mirage, hovered between Lawrence and what his eyes beheld. These things lay before him clear-cut, in their primordial candour, devoid of any veil of suggestion or association. It was his charm. There was something elemental in him, something of the *Erdgeist*.

His genius was pictorial and contemplative, impatient of causes save where the issue was plain to an infant's understanding, as in the matter of that pamphlet on Pornography and Obscenity[1]—a noble pronouncement. Lawrence was no Bohemian; he was a provincial, an inspired provincial with marked puritan leanings. He had a shuddering horror of Casanova's *Memoirs*; he was furious with a friend for keeping two mistresses instead of one, and even with Florentine boys for showing an inch or so of bare flesh above the knee—'I don't like it! I don't like it! Why can't they wear trousers?'; my own improprieties of speech he ascribed to some perverse kink of nature, whereas they were merely an indication of good health. Had he been concerned for his own peace of mind he should have left the department of exact thinking to take care of itself and devoted his energies to that of feeling, for he insisted on discovering ever fresh riddles in the Universe, and these riddles annoyed him. He could flounder in philosophy as few have yet floundered; in his descriptive writings are phrases which none save Lawrence could have struck out. His life was restless, ever moving from place to place. His work moves restlessly from subject to

*From *Looking Back* (New York: Harcourt, 1933) pp. 286–7.

subject, and sometimes, as in certain of his tales, with an enviable flair, an enviable freshness, an enviable mastery.

It is true that, being inwardly consumed and tormented, he never clarified his outlook. Lawrence had neither poise nor reserve. Nor had he a trace of humour. He had courage. He knew what would be the consequence if a notorious book of his should ever be published: a howl of execration. He went ahead.

NOTES

For a note on Norman Douglas see p. 157, n. 1.

1. Lawrence's essay 'Pornography and Obscenity' was published in 1929 and is reprinted in *Phoenix*.

Lawrence as Gossip*

CATHERINE CARSWELL

To read the letters is—as Mr Huxley says of being with their author—'a kind of adventure'. And this, even more than their beauty and absorbing interest, gives them their especial quality. But 'beautiful and absorbingly interesting' they are. And they are also exceedingly amusing. For Lawrence had a tongue. The way he used it was his one vice. Gossip he did, and with what fury! To the deadly venom of a wit that might be termed classical was added a vigour of language acquired from labouring men, and directing these was a ferocity of perception that was all his own. He spoke of people behind their backs as Voltaire must have spoken, or Alexander Pope. But there was this difference, that he had no jealousy in his composition and was as incapable of unkindness as of guile. No man ever desired more truly to see everybody happy and vital up to the measure of their beings. 'I hate my enemies,' he writes in one letter, 'but I mostly forget them.' It was true. And he would never grudge any good that might come to an enemy, though this was not in the sense we understand as Christian, but from an overflowing, impatient life. He was never tolerant, but always sensitive, where others were concerned. Frequently his friends of one day were his enemies of the next, and *vice versa*. It was less at the individual than at some lack of spontaneous life he found there—some

* From 'D. H. Lawrence in his Letters' [review of *The Letters of D. H. Lawrence*], *The Nineteenth Century and After*, cxii (1932) pp. 635–6.

gloomy or glassy unawareness, or some twist excluding life—that he directed his strokes. But the strokes were many and reckless. Those who heard in talk his wild and wicked sketches of the absent were transported with amazement or with laughter or both. You might be incredulous about the portrait-chart—invariably as well as a portrait he gave a chart claiming to reveal the individual's way of life—or shocked or hilarious. But you had to admit its vigour and its originality. Neither could you afterwards survey the subject of it without reference to the incisive outline which, at the time, had appeared to you as exaggerated or merely fantastic. You might still refuse to believe that what Lawrence had said really told you the essential truth about the individual in question. But remembering what he had said, and looking at the individual, you felt that life, including your own, was elucidated and enriched.

It caused, and will continue to cause, trouble. Remarks came, in a version less innocent of spite, to the ears of the person concerned, who became a resentful victim. Lawrence was often called to account. And if he could sometimes confess that he 'rather liked getting into a bit of a mess with people', at other times he swerved violently away from the petty or painful revelations he brought about. Then he cursed himself and others. Yet he would maintain that what he had said was both true in its essence and without malevolence in its intent, and that therefore it could not do anything but good in the end.

NOTE

For a note on Catherine Carswell see p. 97.

The Last Days*

FRIEDA LAWRENCE

Now I am nearing the end...I think of Bandol and our little villa 'Beau Soleil' on the sea, the big balcony windows looking toward the sea, another window at the side overlooking a field of yellow narcissus called 'soleil' and pine-trees beyond and again the sea. I remember sunny days when the waves came flying along with white manes, they looked as if they might come flying right up the terrace into his room. There were plants in his room and they flowered so well and I said to him: 'Why, oh why, can't you

* From *Not I, But the Wind*, pp. 287–96.

flourish like those?' I remember what a beautiful and strange time it was. One day a cat, a big handsome yellow-and-white cat came in; Lawrence chased it away. 'We don't want it. If we go away it'll be miserable. We don't want to take the responsibility for it'; but the cat stayed, it insisted on it. Its name was 'Micky' and it grew more and more beautiful and never a cat played more intelligently than Micky...he played hide-and-go-seek with me, and Lawrence played mouse with him...Lawrence was such a convincing mouse...and then he insisted: 'You must put this cat out at night or it will become a bourgeois, unbeautiful cat.' So very sadly, at nightfall, in spite of Micky's remonstrances I put him out into the garden. To Mme Martens, the cook, Lawrence said: 'Vous lui donnez à manger, il dort avec moi, et Madame l'amuse.'

But in the morning at dawn Micky and I appeared in Lawrence's room...Micky took a flying leap on to Lawrence's bed and began playing with his toes, and I looked at Lawrence to see how he was...his worst time was before dawn when he coughed so much, and I knew what he had been through...But then at dawn I believe he felt grateful that another day had been given him. 'Come when the sun rises,' he said, and when I came he was glad, so very glad, as if he would say: 'See, another day is given me.'

The sun rose magnificently opposite his bed in red and gold across the bay and the fishermen standing up in their boats looked like eternal mythological figures dark and alive against the lit-up splendour of the sea and sky, and when I asked him: 'What kind of a night did you have?' to comfort me, he would answer: 'Not so bad...' but it was bad enough to break one's heart...And his courage and unflinching spirit, doing their level best to live as long as he possibly could in this world he loved so much, gave me courage too. Never, in all illness and suffering, did he let the days sink to a dreary or dull or sordid level...those last months had the glamour of a rosy sunset...I can only think with awe of those last days of his, as of the rays of the setting sun...and the setting sun obliterates all the sordid details of a landscape. So the dreary passages in our lives were wiped out and he said to me: 'Why, oh why did we quarrel so much?' and I could see how it grieved him...our terrible quarrels...but I answered: 'Such as we were, violent creatures, how could we help it?'

One day the charming old mother of Mme Douillet who was at the Hotel Beau Rivage brought us two gold-fish in a bowl; 'Pour amuser Monsieur', but, alas, Micky thought it was 'Pour amuser Monsieur le chat'. With that fixed, incomprehensible cat-stare he watched those red lines moving in the bowl...then my life became an anxious one...the gold-fish had to go in the bathroom on a little table in the sun. Every morning their water was renewed and I had to let it run for half an hour into the bowl. That was all they got, the gold-fish, no food. And they flourished... 'Everything flourishes,' I said to Lawrence imploringly, 'plants and cats and gold-fish, why can't you?' And he said: 'I want to, I want to, I wish I could.'

His friend Earl Brewster[1] came and massaged him every day with coconut oil...and it grieved me to see Lawrence's strong, straight, quick legs gone so thin, so thin...and one day he said to me: 'I could always trust your instinct to know the right thing for me, but now you don't seem to know any more...' I didn't...I didn't know any more...

And one night he asked me: 'Sleep with me', and I did...all night I was aware of his aching inflexible chest, and all night he must have been so sadly aware of my healthy body beside him...always before, when I slept by the side of him, I could comfort and ease him...now no more...He was falling away from life and me, and with all my strength I was helpless...

Micky had his eye on the gold-fish. One sad evening at tea-time the bathroom door was left open...I came and found both gold-fish on the floor, Micky had fished them out of the bowl. I put them in quickly, one revived, a little sadder and less golden for his experience but the other was dead. Lawrence was furious with Micky. 'He knew we wanted him to leave those gold-fish alone, he knew it. We feed him, we take care of him, he had no right to do it.'

When I argued that it was the nature of cats and they must follow their instincts he turned on me and said: 'It's your fault, you spoil him, if he wanted to eat *me* you would let him.' And he wouldn't let Micky come near him for several days.

I felt: 'Now I can do no more for Lawrence, only the sun and the sea and the stars and the moon at night, that's his portion now...' He never would have had the shutters shut or the curtains drawn, so that at night he could see the sky. In those days he wrote his *Apocalypse*;[2] he read it to me, and how strong his voice still was, and I said: 'But this is splendid.'

I was reading the New Testament and told Lawrence: 'I get such a kick out of it, just the same as when Azul gallops like the wind across the desert with me.'

As he read it to me he got angry with all those mixed-up symbols and impossible pictures.

He said: 'In this book I want to go back to old days, pre-Bible days, and pick up for us there what men felt like and lived by then.'

The pure artist in him revolted! His sense of the fitness of things never left him in the lurch! He stuck to his sense of measure and I am often amused at the criticism people bring against him...criticisms only reveal the criticisers and their limitations...If the criticiser is an interesting person his criticism will be interesting, if he isn't then it's waste of time to listen to him. If he voices a general opinion he is uninteresting too, because we all know the general opinion *ad nauseam*. 'My flesh grows weary on my bones' was one of Lawrence's expressions when somebody held forth to him, as if one didn't know beforehand what most people will say!

One day Lawrence said to himself: 'I shan't die...a rich man now...perhaps it's just as well, it might have done something to me.' But I doubt whether even a million or two would have changed him!

One day he said: 'I can't die, I can't die, I hate them too much! I have given too much and what did I get in return?'

It sounded so comical the way he said it, and I ignored the depth of sadness and bitterness of the words and said: 'No, Lawrence, you don't hate them as much as all that.' It seemed to comfort him.

And now I wonder and am grateful for the superhuman strength that was given us both in those days. Deep down I knew 'something is going to happen, we are steering towards some end' but every nerve was strained and every thought and every feeling...Life had to be kept going gaily at any price.

Since Doctor Max Mohr had gone, we had no doctor, only Mme Martens, the cook. She was very good at all kinds of tisanes and inhalations and mustard plasters, and she was a very good cook.

My only grief was that we had no open fireplaces, only central heating and, thank goodness, the sun all day. Lawrence made such wonderful efforts of will to go for walks and the strain of it made him irritable. If I went with him it was pure agony walking to the corner of the little road by the sea, only a few yards! How gallantly he tried to get better and live! He was so very clever with his frail failing body. Again one could learn from him how to handle this complicated body of ours, he knew so well what was good for him, what he needed, by an unfailing instinct, or he would have died many years ago...and I wanted to keep him alive at any cost. I had to see him day by day getting nearer to the end, his spirit so alive and powerful that the end and death seemed unthinkable and always will be, for me.

And then Gertler[3] sent a doctor friend to us, and when he saw Lawrence he said the only salvation was a sanatorium higher up...

For the last years I had found that for a time mountain air, and then a change by the sea, seemed to suit Lawrence best. Lawrence had always thought with horror of a sanatorium, we both thought with loathing of it. Freedom that he cherished so much! He never felt like an invalid, I saw to that! Never should he feel a poor sick thing as long as I was there and his spirit! Now we had to give in...we were beaten. With a set face Lawrence made me bring all his papers on to his bed and he tore most of them up and made everything tidy and neat and helped to pack his own trunks, and I never cried...His self-discipline kept me up, and my admiration for his unfailing courage. And the day came that the motor stood at the door of our little house, Beau Soleil...Micky the cat had been taken by Achsah Brewster. She came before we started with armfuls of almond blossoms, and Earl Brewster travelled with us...And patiently, with a desperate silence, Lawrence set out on his last journey. At Toulon station he had to walk down and up stairs, wasting strength he could ill afford to waste, and the shaking train and then the long drive from Antibes to the 'Ad Astra' at Vence...And again he had to climb stairs. There he lay in a blue room with yellow curtains and great open windows and a balcony looking over the sea. When the doctors examined him and asked him questions about himself he told them: 'I have had bronchitis since I was a fortnight old.'

In spite of his thinness and his illness he never lost his dignity, he fought on and he never lost hope. Friends brought flowers, pink and red cyclamen and hyacinths and fruit...but he suffered much and when I bade him 'good night' he said: 'Now I shall have to fight several battles of Waterloo before morning.' I dared not understand to the full the meaning of his words. One day he said to my daughter:

'Your mother does not care for me any more, the death in me is repellent to her.'

But it was the sadness of his suffering...and he would not eat and he had much pain...and we tried so hard to think of different foods for him. His friends tried to help him, the Di Chiaras[4] and the Brewsters and Aldous and Maria Huxley and Ida Rauh.[5]

Wells came to see him, and the Aga Khan[6] with his charming wife. Jo Davidson did a bust of him.[7]

One night I saw how he did not want me to go away, so I came again after dinner and I said: 'I'll sleep in your room tonight.' His eyes were so grateful and bright, but he turned to my daughter and said: 'It isn't often I want your mother, but I do want her tonight to stay.' I slept on the long chair in his room, and I looked out at the dark night and I wanted one single star to shine and comfort me, but there wasn't one; it was a dark big sky, and no moon and no stars. I knew how Lawrence suffered and yet I could not help him. So the days went by in agony and the nights too; my legs would hardly carry me, I could not stay away from him, and always the dread, 'How shall I find him?' One night I thought of the occasion long ago when I knew I loved him, when a tenderness for him rose in me that I had not known before. He had taken my two little girls and me for a walk in Sherwood Forest, through some fields we walked, and the children ran all over the place, and we came to a brook...it ran rather fast under a small stone bridge. The children were thrilled, the brook ran so fast. Lawrence quite forgot me but picked daisies and put them face upwards on one side of the bridge in the water and then said: 'Now look, look if they come out on the other side.'

He also made them paper boats and put burning matches into them; 'this is the Spanish Armada, and you don't know what that was'. 'Yes, we do,' the older girl said promptly. I can see him now, crouching down, so intent on the game, so young and quick, and the small girls in their pink and white striped Viyella frocks, long-legged like colts, in wild excitement over such a play-fellow. But that was long ago...and I thought: 'This is the man whom they call sex-obsessed.'

I slept on his cane chair several nights. I heard coughing from many rooms, old coughing and young coughing. Next to his room was a young girl with her mother, and I heard her call out: 'Mama, Mama, je souffre tant!' I was glad Lawrence was a little deaf and could not hear it all. One day he tried to console me and said: 'You must not feel so sympathetic for people. When people are ill or have lost their eyesight there is always a compensation. The state they are in is different. You needn't think it's the same as when you are well.'

After one night when he had suffered so much, I told myself: 'It is enough, it is enough; nobody should have to stand this.'

He was very irritable and said: 'Your sleeping here does me no good.' I ran away and wept. When I came back he said so tenderly: 'Don't mind, you know I want nothing but you, but sometimes something is stronger in me.'

We prepared to take him out of the nursing home and rented a villa where we took him...It was the only time he allowed me to put on his shoes, everything else he always did for himself. He went in the shaking taxi and he was taken into the house and lay down on the bed on which he was to die, exhausted. I slept on the couch where he could see me. He still ate. The next day was a Sunday. 'Don't leave me,' he said, 'don't go away'. So I sat by his bed and read. He was reading the life of Columbus. After lunch he began to suffer very much and about tea-time he said: 'I must have a temperature, I am delirious. Give me the thermometer.' This is the only time, seeing his tortured face, that I cried, and he said: 'Don't cry', in a quick, compelling voice. So I ceased to cry any more. He called Aldous and Maria Huxley who were there, and for the first time he cried out to them in his agony. 'I ought to have some morphine now,' he told me and my daughter, so Aldous went off to find a doctor to give him some...Then he said: 'Hold me, hold me, I don't know where I am, I don't know where my hands are...where am I?'

Then the doctor came and gave him a morphine injection. After a little while he said: 'I am better now, if I could only sweat I would be better...' and then again: 'I am better now.' The minutes went by, Maria Huxley was in the room with me. I held his left ankle from time to time, it felt so full of life, all my days I shall hold his ankle in my hand.

He was breathing more peacefully, and then suddenly there were gaps in the breathing. The moment came when the thread of life tore in his heaving chest, his face changed, his cheeks and jaw sank, and death had taken hold of him...Death was there, Lawrence was dead. So simple, so small a change, yet so final, so staggering. Death!

I walked up and down beside his room, by the balcony, and everything looked different, there was a new thing, death, where there had been life, such intense life. The olive trees outside looked so black and close, and the sky so near; I looked into the room, there were his slippers with the shape of his feet standing neatly under the bed, and under the sheet he lay, cold and remote, he whose ankle I had held alive only an hour or so ago...I looked at his face. So proud, manly and splendid he looked, a new face there was. All suffering had been wiped from it, it was as if I had never seen him or known him in all the completeness of his being. I wanted to touch him but dared not, he was no longer in life with me. There had been the change, he belonged somewhere else now, to all the elements; he was the earth and sky, but no longer a living man. Lawrence, my Lorenzo who had loved me and I him...he was dead...

Then we buried him, very simply, like a bird we put him away, a few of us who loved him. We put flowers into his grave and all I said was: 'Good-bye, Lorenzo', as his friends and I put lots and lots of mimosa on his coffin. Then he was covered over with earth while the sun came out on to his small grave in the little cemetery of Vence which looks over the Mediterranean that he cared for so much.

NOTES

For a note on Frieda Lawrence see p. 88.

1. See p. 159.
2. Published posthumously in 1931.
3. See p. 112, n. 4.
4. An American couple who had known Lawrence in Capri.
5. Ida Rauh (Mrs Max Eastman) was an American actress for whom Lawrence had written his play *David* (1925).
6. The Moslem leader (1877–1957).
7. American sculptor; the clay head of Lawrence which he made in February 1930 is reproduced in Harry T. Moore and Warren Roberts, *D. H. Lawrence and His World* (London: Thames and Hudson, 1966) p. 125.

The Last Days:
Another Account*

BARBARA WEEKLEY BARR

In the winter of 1928–9, Lawrence and Frieda were staying at the Hôtel Beau Rivage, at Bandol in the French Riviera. I spent a fortnight there just after Christmas when I was in a miserable, nervous state. Lawrence was very ill himself. It was an agonising time.

Frieda had been in tears on Christmas Day, Lawrence told me, because she did not have a single present.

* From 'Memoir of D. H. Lawrence', in *D. H. Lawrence: Novelist, Poet, Prophet*, ed. Spender, pp. 30–6.

'There she was, howling like an infant,' he said contemptuously. To cheer herself up, she had put a photograph of Monty on a shelf, but Lawrence took it away, saying that to have photographs about was vulgar. A little while later he had burst out, 'Why don't your children send you presents?'

After he went to his bedroom, which led off Frieda's, we would hear his continual cough. During the day he looked exhausted and ill.

He had just finished his *Pansies* poems, and before sending them off to his London publisher, he read them to us as we sat on Frieda's bed. These bitter poems had the effect of clearing my suffocated mind.

When Lawrence had gone to bed, I said to Frieda, 'He promised to make a new heaven and earth for your children when you went away together. Well, it's true; he has.' Frieda told me later that she had repeated this to Lawrence, and he had been pleased.

A young American[1] from California, who was at Oxford, met us in the street at Bandol.

'Are you D. H. Lawrence?' he asked. He explained that he was looking for the 'ultimate reality'.

Lawrence invited him to come back to the hotel with us where, sitting in Frieda's bedroom, they threshed it out. Alas! The discussion was over my head.

'There *is* no ultimate reality,' said Lawrence, firmly, after a time. I doubted if this satisfied the young man. Soon after the American took me out to tea, and told me I was bad for Lawrence's genius and had better go away.

'He is mad, madder even than you are, Barby,' said Lawrence. 'He hates Oxford even more than you do your set-up. But you are both in a state of hate, and have got yourselves on the brain...It's a common form of hysteria. You used to have a rather amusing temper that popped up now and then like a little devil, or Jack-in-the-box. Now it's got hold of you completely. You are cynical as well. That's dreadful.'

After a few days the news came that the *Pansies* had been seized by the police in the post. This upset Lawrence painfully. The feeling of tension increased, and there seemed a malaise in the hotel.

We had arranged to meet a friend of mine, Cynthia Kent, in Cannes, but in our distraction we went on the wrong day. As Cynthia failed to appear, Lawrence, suspecting some fresh insult, became frantically annoyed.

Lawrence was relieved when a cheerful colonial he knew wrote that he was coming to pay him a visit. 'Now don't say anything, but I think Barby might like him,' he said to Frieda. I think this was Lawrence's only attempt at matchmaking for me.

The young man, who was called Stephenson, proved a jolly, go-ahead sort of person. Something he had seen in a night club had given him an idea for a short story. He sat down almost as soon as he arrived and 'got it off his chest'. It was about an older woman leading a beautiful young woman astray. He read it to us as we all sat, as usual, in Frieda's bedroom. When he had finished, Lawrence demolished it for him at once.

'It's false,' he told him. 'It wouldn't convince anybody. The emotions and situations are quite unreal. You'll have to re-write it.'

'He is *not* an artist; he is a businessman,' he told Frieda afterwards. 'Why does everyone try to write? I don't see there's so much fun in it.'

Lawrence worried about me; my depression effected him. He was rather tired now by my endless dilemmas.

'I had a dreadful dream,' he told us one morning. 'I was rescuing Barby from some disaster. She was in a fearful fix as usual.'

When I was returning to England, Frieda said, 'If you can't stand it, you can come out to us at Majorca.' That was to be their next resting-place. I believe it was from Majorca that Lawrence wrote to me: 'I think that your headaches may be due to a deep change in the psyche, and you will just have to lie low and bear the change. Don't make too many efforts, especially efforts with people, and don't try to paint at present. Later on you might be really worthwhile.'

In the winter of 1929, I had a letter from Frieda from a villa they had taken at Bandol called the 'Beau Soleil'. Lawrence was now extremely ill and spent a good deal of time in bed. People were trying to persuade him to go into a sanatorium. 'They say he must have a nurse. He says, "Can't I have Barby?" ' she wrote. This pleased me, and I went out to Bandol, arriving there one winter evening.

The Beau Soleil was a little box of a villa near the sea.

Lawrence was sitting up in bed, wearing a blue cloth jacket. A ginger cat was sleeping on his bed, making him look quite homely.

After supper we sorted out some papers together. 'Don't yawn, Barby, it's boring!' he said, engrossed.

'The nights are so awful,' he told me. 'At two in the morning, if I had a pistol I would shoot myself.'

Sometimes Lawrence walked feebly into the garden, and lay on a chaise-longue. He felt Frieda could not help him any more, and this made him resentful. Covered with rugs, and lying in the garden with a grey, drawn expression on his face, he said, 'Your mother is repelled by the death in me.'

Some Americans came to see him. Lawrence said the wife was going mad because she had tried to insist on the ideal of goodness and beauty. The proprietress of the hotel came and chatted with him in her bright French way, but she, too, got on his nerves.

The person who seemed to tire him least was the cook's cracked old husband, who would come and stand at the foot of his bed, waving his peaked cap, talking inconsequentially, and laughing like a noodle.

A young doctor from an English sanatorium came to see him with his consumptive wife. Lawrence liked her. 'She is like all people with chest trouble...gives too much life away,' he remarked.

I cooked some of Lawrence's meals, especially his breakfast, because he liked porridge. Frieda found me a little 'managing', I think, a little like Ada.

We all three decided to go to the ranch in New Mexico for which Lawrence longed, believing he could recover there. Frieda thought that I could go out first, and stay with Mabel Luhan.

Lawrence was amazed at this suggestion. 'What on earth do you think that Mabel would want with Frieda's daughter?' he demanded. 'You might just as well throw Barby into the sea!'

'But if you and your mother really could love each other,' he said to me later, 'you might make a life together.'

In early February, Lawrence had left Bandol for the Ad Astra sanatorium at Vence in the Maritime Alps. Frieda went with him; I stayed on at the Villa Beau Soleil.

A friend of mine met them at Nice, and motored them to the sanatorium.

'Blair [Hughes-Stanton][2] has been as kind as an angel to me,' wrote Lawrence from there, adding, 'Here is £10 for housekeeping.' To this Frieda put a postscript. 'Be careful with the money.' This admonition impressed me so much, that when Blair and his wife came to see me, I gave them only a few rags of boiled meat from the soup for lunch, and offended them.

A little later I joined Frieda in Vence where she was staying at the Hotel Nouvel. When I went to see Lawrence at the sanatorium, I found him worse. In his balcony room, painted a dreary blue, he seemed wretchedly ill and wasted. For the first few days he had gone downstairs for lunch, but the other patients depressed him.

The superintendent was a cheerless person. 'Monsieur Lawrence is a lamp that is slowly failing,' he said to me unctuously.

Lawrence wanted to leave and go into a villa somewhere near. We had difficulty in finding this, because the French, often so reckless, seem terrified of invalids. Many whom I approached refused to let their villas on that account. At least we found the Villa Robermond on the hill just above Vence. It was a comfortable house, with a little cottage where an Italian peasant lived with his wife, who acted as concierge.

Lawrence still thought that if he could rest, and regain a little strength, he might be able to travel to New Mexico. To go there had also become my dream. In Nice I made enquiries about our passports.

Before Lawrence left the sanatorium several people visited him there. H. G. Wells, whom he did not like, came one afternoon, and told him his illness was mainly hysteria. The Aga Khan and his wife also came, and the Aga cheered Lawrence by saying he admired his paintings.

Lawrence complained to him of the way his work had been treated, and said: 'The English kill all their poets off by the time they are forty.'

Before taking Lawrence from the sanatorium, we engaged an English nurse. We also found another doctor, a Corsican, who was recommended by an American friend.

On 1 March, Lawrence drove up to the Villa Robermond with Frieda in a taxi. I saw him, in hat and overcoat, stagger up the few steps of the verandah, supported by the chauffeur. He was saying, 'I am very ill.'

After he was put to bed, the new doctor examined him. When he came out of Lawrence's room, he said, 'It is very grave. There is not much hope. Do not let him see that you know.' To our American friend Ida Eastman,[3] he said, 'He is simply living on his spirit.'

The next morning Lawrence got up, washed, and brushed his teeth. He did not care much for the ministrations of the nurse, though she was unobtrusive enough, poor thing.

'She is so insipid,' he whispered. She was very unhappy, and sulked a good deal.

Lawrence said he thought he should rewrite the will he had once made but lost, in which he left everything to Frieda; but she feared it would tire him too much.

I cooked Lawrence's lunch, and took it in to find him sitting up in the blue jacket, tranquilly reading a book about Columbus's voyage to America.

The Huxleys came in the afternoon, and the nurse voiced her woes to Maria. Towards evening Lawrence suddenly became worse. His head began to distress him. Sitting up in agony, holding his head, Lawrence cried, 'I must have morphia.'

I put my arm round him for a few moments. I could not understand why the doctor had not come, and decided to go for him. When I left, Lawrence said to my mother, 'Put your arm round me like Barby did; it made me feel better.'

As I was leaving to go to Vence, Aldous and Maria came again from their hotel. Maria went and soothed Lawrence, holding his head in her hands. He had said she had his mother's hands.

He sat up in bed with startled brilliant eyes, looking across the room, crying, 'I see my body over there on the table!'

When I reached the Corsican doctor's house, I found that he had gone to Nice, so I hurried with a friend to the Hotel Nouvel. There the proprietor telephoned to the superintendent of the sanatorium, asking him to come and give Lawrence morphia. This was a lengthy talk, as the doctor at first refused. At last the proprietor won him round, so we called for him in a car and took him up to the villa. He complained all the way.

When we arrived there, however, his professional manner asserted itself. He greeted Lawrence kindly, and his greeting was returned. He gave him morphia, and left.

Aldous Huxley thought we had better go to Vence and try again to find the Corsican doctor, in case the effect of the injection wore off. We went to his house, but he was still away. It was about eleven at night when we walked up the hill to the villa again, talking of Lawrence and his illness. We found Frieda and Maria in the kitchen, with the peasant of the conciergerie standing by.

'We could not get the doctor,' I told them agitatedly.

'It doesn't matter,' said Frieda, gently.

Three days later, a light hearse carrying Lawrence's coffin was drawn to Vence cemetery by a small black horse, which picked its way intelligently down the rough hillside. Two wild-looking men accompanied it.

Robert Nichols,[4] Achsah Brewster, the Huxleys, Frieda and I went to the grave. The English chaplain at Vence had sent a message, saying if he could be allowed to come and say one or two prayers, he would waive the usual burial service. This offer was refused. There was no religious rite.

The head of Lawrence's grave was against a sunny wall. One could see the Mediterranean far away below, and nearer, the dignified cypresses.

Two young Italians were commissioned to make a mosaic phoenix for the headstone. They worked it in pebbles of rose, white, and gray. Sometimes we watched these two, Domenique and Nicola, at work.

One day a tall dark woman came into the cemetery but, seeing us, went away. This was the 'Louie'[5] of Lawrence's early days. They had been engaged for a short time, but he had broken it off, telling her, 'You see, I don't think we could make a life together.' A fortnight later he met Frieda.

Speaking once of her he said, 'She was dark, good-looking. I liked her and she attracted me very much physically. But I didn't live with her, because she would have given too much—it wouldn't have been fair. I would like to do something for Louie one day.'

After we had left the cemetery, she came back and left some flowers there. On her return to the Midlands she wrote to Ada: 'I went to Vence and saw the poor lad's grave.'

A few weeks after Lawrence's death Frieda went to London to see to her affairs. I stayed on alone at the villa. At night the peasant's dog slept on the floor by my bed for company. I never shut the door of Lawrence's room across the salon, thinking that if there should be an after-life, his spirit might like to go in and out of it.

*   *   *

[*Later she was seriously ill with bronchitis.*]

When I was getting better, I lay in bed one bright autumn morning and Frieda came in, bringing Lawrence's early letters to her for me to read. I picked one up and began, but halfway through, feeling listless, wretched, and confused, put it down again. At that moment I clearly saw Lawrence's image bending over me. It was made up of little shimmering particles. His form was filled out, glowing, and he looked at me with a very benign expression. I blinked, startled by the vision: it vanished and, to my regret, never appeared again.

NOTES

For a note on Barbara Barr see p. 90.

1. Probably Brewster Ghiselin (see p. 262).

2. English painter and wood-engraver who had executed the illustrations for two volumes of Lawrence's poems.

3. See p. 283, n. 5.

4. See p. 109, n. 11.

5. Louise Burrows lived near Ilkeston, Derbyshire, and met Lawrence whilst he was attending the Pupil-teacher Centre there in 1903–5. Lawrence proposed to her in December 1910, but their engagement was short-lived. Ursula Brangwen in *The Rainbow* is said to have been partly based on her. See *Lawrence in Love: Letters to Louie Burrows*, ed. James T. Boulton (Nottingham: University of Nottingham Press, 1968).

Some Letters and an Interview*

ALDOUS HUXLEY

From a letter to Leonard Huxley, June 1927

We went to Florence the other day to see our poor friend D. H. Lawrence, the novelist, who was down with a nasty attack of haemorrhage from the lungs—long-standing tuberculosis, which has suddenly taken a turn for the worse. This is decidedly not a temperature to be ill in, and the poor wretch is not strong enough, nor secure enough from fresh bleedings, to move away from Florence into the cool of the mountains. He was with us at Forte, some three or four weeks ago, and I am afraid that bathing did him no good. The first attack came on shortly after he had left us. He is a very

* From *The Letters of Aldous Huxley*, ed. Grover Smith (London: Chatto & Windus, 1969) pp. 288, 313–14, 330–1, 332; *Writers at Work: the 'Paris Review' Interviews, Second Series*, ed. George Plimpton (New York: Viking Press, 1963) pp. 209–10.

extraordinary man, for whom I have a great admiration and liking—but difficult to get on with, passionate, queer, violent. However, age is improving him and now his illness has cured him of his violences and left him touchingly gentle. I hope profoundly he'll get over this business. The doctor seemed to think he'd be all right; but with these haemorrhages one can never be quite certain. A particularly violent bout of bleeding can happen, even when the patient seems to be getting much better, and the end can be quite sudden and unexpected.

From a letter to Julian Huxley, 13 July 1929

Lawrence was here a few days and is gone again. If you knew the struggles we had had with him about his health—but quite in vain. When he was in Paris, before he went to Majorca, we actually got him to agree to undertake a treatment, alone, *minus* Frieda, and we also actually got him to go to a doctor in Paris. He was to go back to the doctor to be X-rayed. (Meanwhile, however, the doctor told M[1] that, from just sounding him, he could hear that one lung was practically gone and the other affected. He doubted whether very much could be done.) Then Frieda, who had been in London, returned. L felt himself reinforced. He refused to go back to the doctor, refused to think of the treatment and set off with Frieda (of whom he had bitterly complained when he was alone with us) to Majorca. So that's that. It's no good. He doesn't *want* to know how ill he is: that, I believe, is the fundamental reason why he won't go to doctors and homes. He only went in Paris because he was feeling iller than usual and was even more frightened of dying at once than of hearing how ill he was. He rationalises the fear in all kinds of ways which are, of course, quite irrelevant. And meantime he just wanders about, very tired and at bottom wretched, from one place to another, imagining that the next place will make him feel better and, when he gets [to] the next place, regretting the one before and looking back on it as a paradise. But of course no place will make him feel any better than any other now that he's as ill as he is. He's a great deal worse than he was when you saw him at Diablerets—coughs more, breathes very quickly and shallowly, has no energy. (It's pathetic to see the way he just sits and does nothing. He hasn't written a line or painted a stroke for the last 3 months. Just lack of vital strength.) He still talks a good deal and can get amused and excited into the semblance of health for an hour or two at a time. But it is only a semblance, I'm afraid. I think he's even worse than he was in Paris in March (when he had a touch of flu to complicate matters). The doctor told M that he might drag on for quite a little time like this, unless he got a cold which turned into bronchitis or pneumonia, when he'd simply be asphyxiated. He has gone to Germany now—or is just going: for he has been in Florence these last days—of all places in this weather! We have given up trying to persuade him to be reasonable. He doesn't want to be and no one can persuade him to be—except possibly Frieda. But Frieda is worse than he is. We've told her that she's a fool and a criminal; but it has no more effect than telling an elephant. So it's hopeless. Short of handcuffing him and taking him to a sanatorium by force, there's nothing to be done.

From a letter to Julian Huxley, 3 March 1930

As you will have seen by the papers, DHL died yesterday. We had just got back from Villefranche, where we had been seeing the Nicholses over the weekend, and found him very weak and suffering much pain and strangely *égaré*, feeling that he wasn't there—that he was two people at once. We got the doctor up at nine, who stuck some morphia into him, and he settled off to sleep—to die quietly at 10.15. The heart had begun to go and the intestines were badly affected—general intoxication, I suppose—and he seemed to have hardly any lungs left to breathe with. It had been most distressing, the two or three times we saw him during the past week—he was such a miserable wreck of himself and suffering so much pain. Moreover the illness had reduced him to an appalling state of emaciation. So that it was a great comfort really that he went when he did—and went so quietly at the last. The funeral takes place tomorrow at Vence.

From a letter to Eugene F. Saxton, 8 March 1930

I would have written earlier if these last two weeks had not been so fully and painfully occupied with the illness and death of our poor friend D. H. Lawrence. We came down to see him a fortnight ago and found him even worse than we had expected to find him, and terribly changed from what he was—and he was already a very sick man even then—when we last saw him in the Summer. He gave one the impression that he was living by sheer force of will and by nothing else. But the dissolution of the body was breaking down the will. The end came on Sunday night. He was really, I think, the most extraordinary and impressive human being I have ever known.

From an interview, c. 1960

INTERVIEWERS: Now, thirty years later, would you care to say what you think of Lawrence as a novelist and as a man?
HUXLEY: I occasionally reread some of his books. How good he is! Especially in the short stories. And the other day I read part of *Women in Love*, and that again seemed very good. The vividness, the incredible vividness of the descriptions of nature is amazing in Lawrence. But

sometimes one doesn't know what he's getting at. In *The Plumed Serpent*, for instance, he'll glorify the Mexican Indians with their dark life of the blood on one page, and then on the next he'll damn the lazy natives like a British colonel in the days of Kipling. That book is a mass of contradictions. I was very fond of Lawrence as a man. I knew him very well the last four years of his life. I had met him during the First World War and saw him a certain amount then, but I didn't get to know him really well till 1926. I was a little disturbed by him. You know, he *was* rather disturbing. And to a conventionally brought up young bourgeois he was rather difficult to understand. But later on I got to know and like him. My first wife became very friendly with him and understood him and they got on very well together. We saw the Lawrences often during those last four years; they stayed with us in Paris, then we were together in Switzerland, and we visited them at the Villa Mirenda near Florence. My wife typed out the manuscript of *Lady Chatterley's Lover* for him, even though she was a bad typist and had no patience with English spelling—she was a Belgian, you know. Then she didn't always appreciate the nuances of the language she was typing. When she started using some of those four-letter words in conversation, Lawrence was profoundly shocked.

INTERVIEWERS: Why did Lawrence keep moving around so much?

HUXLEY: One reason he was forever moving on is that his relations with people would become so complicated that he'd have to get away. He was a man who loved and hated too intensely; he both loved and hated the same people at the same time. Then, like a great many tubercular people, he was convinced that climate had a great effect on him—not only the temperature, but the direction of the wind, and all sorts of atmospheric conditions. He had invented a whole mythology of climate. In his last years he wanted to go back to New Mexico. He had been very happy there on the ranch in Taos. But he wasn't strong enough to make the trip. By all the rules of medicine he should have been dead; but he lived on, supported by some kind of energy that seemed to be independent of his body. And he kept on writing to the end...We were there, in Vence, when he died...He actually died in my first wife's arms.

NOTES

For a note on Aldous Huxley see p. 123. A few days after Lawrence's death Huxley wrote that he had 'discussed the question of a biography with Mrs Lawrence and we have come to the conclusion that it is still too early to write a life of DHL as it should be written—quite truthfully' (*Letters of Aldous Huxley*, p. 331). Huxley proposed a memorial volume in which Lawrence's letters would be interspersed with recollections by those who had known him at various stages of his life. This project was abandoned, but Huxley's edition of the letters was later published by Heinemann.

1. Maria Huxley.

Obituary *

JOHN MIDDLETON MURRY

Lawrence was the most remarkable and most lovable man I have ever known. Contact with him was immediate, intimate, and rich. A radiance of warm life streamed from him. When he was gay, and he was often gay— my dominant memory of him is of a blithe and joyful man—he seemed to spread a sensuous enchantment about him. By a natural magic he unsealed the eyes of those in his company: birds, beasts, and flowers became new-minted as in Paradise; they stood revealed as what they were, and not the poor objects of our dull and common seeing. The most ordinary domestic act—the roasting of a joint of meat, the washing-up of crockery, the painting of a cottage room—in his doing became a gay sacrament. He surrendered himself completely to whatever he had in hand; he was utterly engrossed by it. And the things he took in hand were innumerable. In bare record they may seem fantastic, as when for weeks together he decorated little wooden boxes, or, years later when, during his last Christmas in England, he fashioned a marvellous little Adam and Eve beneath the tree in Eden, made of modelling clay and painted; but those who shared in these makings will remember them for some of the most simple, happy hours in their lives.

As his happiness was radiant, so his gloom was a massive darkness in which his intimates were engulfed. I see him sitting crouched and collapsed on a wooden chair when the long horror of the war had begun to gnaw his vitals—forlorn, silent, dead. One could not speak against the numbness of that sheer desolation. But sometimes, in those bitter days—out of which sprang his lifelong passion of rebellion against the European consciousness, and his unresting search for a land and a way of life to which he could surrender himself—sometimes, in those days he would rise to the surface with a flickering smile and begin to sing:

> Sometimes, I feel like an eagle in the sky...
> Sometimes, I feel like a moaning dove...

With the first line he soared; with the second he sank down, down, down.

He was completely generous. At a moment when there were not ten

* *Times Literary Supplement*, 13 Mar 1930, p. 208 (unsigned).

pounds between him and destitution he thrust five of them upon a friend and, because the friend refused them, flew into a transport of high-pitched rage. Friendship was to him a blood-brotherhood, an absolute and inviolable loyalty, but not to a person, but to the impersonal godhead beneath. I do not believe that he ever found the friendship after which he hungered; and perhaps this was the tragedy of his life. The men he knew were incapable of giving that which he demanded. It was not their fault, though in his heart of hearts he believed it was.

He had an infinite capacity for making warm human contacts. In whatever part of the world he found himself in his quest for newness of life, he left his mark and memory among the common people. Whatever may be our intellectual judgement of the theories he built upon his immediate experience, no one who knew him well has any doubt whatever that he had a mysterious gift of 'sensing' the hidden and unconscious reality of his fellow human beings. He did not sentimentalise about them, but he did *know* them, in ways more direct and ultimate than any of which ordinary men have experience. What is vague and dimly apprehended instinct with most of us was in him an exquisitely ramified sensibility, responsive to realities which elude our blunter organisations and for which our common language has no appropriate expression. Hence the seeming violence which Lawrence, a native master of the delicate and creative word, did to the conventions of style and morality. His sacrifice of 'art' was quite conscious, and quite deliberate; he was not concerned with it any more. 'Fiction,' he said in a letter, 'is about *persons*; and I am not interested in persons.'

Perhaps he never clearly understood how extraordinary were these gifts of his for making contact with the life that is prior to personality. No doubt for a man of genius such as his to admit that he is in some sense radically unlike his fellows—a queer creature, an animal of a different species—is almost impossible. Such absolute isolation is not to be endured. Because Lawrence found his friends and mankind at large lacking in faculties which were native to him, he inclined to believe that they had deliberately buried in the earth a talent which was never theirs. So he was often, in his later years, induced to think men perverse and wicked when they were merely dull; and he grew exasperated with them.

NOTE

For a note on J. M. Murry, see p. 133. Murry reproduced this obituary notice at the end of his *Reminiscences of D. H. Lawrence.*

'A Man of Destiny'*

JOHN MIDDLETON MURRY

So, Lawrence, you died. 'Even the dead,' you wrote of Maurice Magnus, 'ask only for *justice*.'[1] But what is justice? 'Anger,' you wrote again, 'is just, and pity is just; but judgement is never just.' Shall we be angry with you then, or shall we pity you? Would even pity bring balm to your uneasy ghost?

Neither anger, nor pity, nor judgement is just. There is only one justice in the world worth having, and it is neither anger, nor pity, nor judgement, but the simple understanding which is love indeed: the understanding which accepts the things that are in all the beauty of their manifest necessity.

The evil that you did, is done; and it *is* evil. You muddied the spring of living water that flowed in you more richly than in any man of your time. In the world of good and evil, wherein men must struggle for ever while they live, you quenched the light more often than you kindled it. You bewildered men who might have learned from you, betrayed men who would have followed you. We needed a leader and a prophet, you were marked by destiny to be the man; and you failed us. It was your destiny to fail us, as it was your destiny to fail yourself. In the measure in which you failed yourself, you failed your fellow-men.

But there is a world beyond the world of good and evil: the eternal world of Being, whose reality you denied, known by the Spirit, which you would not suffer to lodge within yourself. In that world you are a perfect thing, which those who understood must love, and those who love must understand. In that world, love and understanding are one. Neither is possible there without the other.

This understanding, so far as I am capable of it, I have given you in this book. In life you asked something of me which was not in my power to give, nor in your power to take. I did not know what it was you asked of me, neither did you know. But I know now. I remember how, one night, when you had returned to England, after all the pain of separation and the torment of love that had turned to hatred, you became to me once more the wonderful Man: superhuman by the anguish and excess of your humanity.

* From *Son of Woman: The Story of D. H. Lawrence* (London: Jonathan Cape, 1931) pp. 387–9.

Suddenly, you put your arm about my neck, for the first and the last time, and said: 'Do not betray me!'[2] I did not understand, but I never forgot. The words, and the suffering in the words, have never ceased to echo in my soul.

In this book have I betrayed you? Was it this, that I have done, of which you were afraid? There was nothing to fear. This 'betrayal' was the one thing you lacked, the one thing I had to give, that you might shine forth among men as the thing of wonder that you were.

For truly you were wonderful among the sons of men, and you gave the world a gift beyond price: not a gift of prophecy or wisdom, for truth and falsehood are mingled to utter confusion in your work—but the gift of yourself. Without someone to 'betray' you, it could never have been given. No man in these latter days has given to men so marvellous or so terrible a picture of Man as you have given. No such picture of Man existed in the world before you came. You were a man of destiny, driven to sacrifice yourself in order that men might know themselves, and the eternal laws they must obey, the laws which, even in denying them, still they obey. Two eternal things you denied, two things of which the promise was richer in you than in any other man whom living men have known: Love and the Spirit, which cannot exist apart. You denied them to the end. Yet to those two things your appeal will be enduring. That which you sought to strangle, you are doomed to bring to birth, in men.

NOTES

For a note on J. Middleton Murry, see p. 133.
1. See p. 157, n. 4.
2. For earlier accounts of this incident, see pp. 196, 198.

'A Man in Bondage'*

JESSIE CHAMBERS

. . . your book[1] will rank along with the other Laurentian literature; it is a document; and if it bears witness rather to the author than to the subject of the work, it is not the less interesting and significant. I can't wax enthusiastic about it, because it is concerned with that aspect of DHL that

* From '"ET" on D. H. Lawrence: A Letter to a Common Friend', *Arena*, 1 (1950) pp. 61–5.

I have always found least interesting. As an artist, when he is dealing with the immediate and concrete, he is superb, but when he assays to be a thinker, I find him superficial and unconvincing, and quite soon boring. The Revelation of John of Patmos, and *Apocalypse* of DHL, can never have any but a secondary interest for me. I have never been able to read the biblical Revelations—when I have tried, I have soon felt that here was the basis for all the Old Moore's Almanacs that ever existed, and the guesses and speculations and the monstrous beasts are only wearisome. As a fragmentary and mutilated account of mankind's early attempts to understand his place in the universe, it *is* interesting, but that was not really DHL's concern with Revelations. His concern was to find some means of escape from that narrow prison of his own ego, and to do so he was prepared to assault the cosmos. So, whenever I read his almost delirious denunciations of what he pretended to regard as Christianity I only see the caged panther lashing himself into a fury to find some way out of his strait prison.

DHL was a man in bondage and all his theorisings and philosophisings only bear witness to his agony. The more I ponder upon his life and his death, the more significant becomes to me the fact of his suffering—of course I don't mean his physical suffering, *that* was the direct outcome of his spiritual anguish at his own frustration. Well, why was he frustrated, and why was he in bondage? Some of his own words come to my mind. The day before his mother's funeral we went a walk together, and during that walk I reproached him for having become engaged to X. I said: 'You ought not to have involved X in the tangle of our relationship.'...DHL's reply took my breath away; he said...'With *should* and *ought* I have nothing to do.' If you will think out the implications of that statement you will see what was the nature of DHL's bondage; he was the measure of his own universe; his own god—and also his own hell. He deliberately (or perhaps he couldn't help it)—anyhow, he regarded himself as exempt from the laws that hold mankind together (I am not referring to conventional morality) and when a human being does that, he is of necessity cut off from contact with his fellows. It seemed to me that DHL's great powers—far from exempting him from responsibility, conferred upon him a much greater and higher order of responsibility. I could only think that time would prove. At the end of that same walk, as we stood within a stone's throw of the house where his mother lay dead, he said to me:

'You know J, I've always loved mother.'

'I know you have,' I replied.

'I don't mean that,' he answered. 'I've loved her—like a lover—that's why I could never love you.'

Then he handed me the three poems[2] he had written since she had died. I think this partly explains why he had placed himself beyond ordinary human sanctions. He was, as it were, driven out of the land of the living into a fearful wilderness of egoism. It explains, too, why, as you remark in your book, he looked in woman only for the animal—female—qualities. It made his dilemma a cruel one, because it compelled him to deny what was best in himself. Consequently his prison was also a terrible battleground where his two selves were constantly fighting each other.

I'll tell you one other incident. On the day when he first met Mrs Weekley at lunch, he came to tea at the Farm here; and after tea, in the parlour, he said to me in accents of despair:

'When we are not together, since we have been parted, I'm not the same man. I don't think the same, feel the same: *I* can't write poetry.' There was his dilemma; one DHL saw one thing with intense clarity; the other went the way of a doomed man. As he said so often; he couldn't help it. But what a price he paid.

I don't propose to write a book about him, and yet I know an aspect of his life that no one else has ever known or can possibly know. So I hope to leave a simple historical record of all I know about him, so that if at some future time some biographer with no pre-conceived theories about him, but a genuine desire to find out what manner of man he was, and what forces went to his making, should arise, my record will exist as one of the 'sources'. That, I feel, I owe to DHL and to what he stood for. But I loathe exhibitionism, so that only a later generation will read my record, if indeed it is ever read.

Strangely enough, the record will extend just beyond his death, and perhaps you will be interested to hear that part. As I have said, the fact of DHL's suffering is the dominant fact in his life for me, and it was only after the publication of *The Plumed Serpent* that I realised he was a tortured spirit. As you know, I returned his last letter in 1913, and since then no word ever passed between us, and I never heard news of him; his name was never mentioned to me. I did not know he was ill; the letter he sent to David[3] was never shown to me until weeks after his death, so that whatever knowledge I had of him came through other channels than those of ordinary communication. For some eighteen months or so before his death I felt acutely drawn to him at times, and wondered intensely how some kind of communication that seemed so urgently needed, was to be established. It seemed to be not just a matter of writing a letter—something else, something different was needed. The feeling that some drawing together was imminent scarcely ever left me. Once quite suddenly, as though he had spoken, the words came into my mind—'We are still on the same planet.' There were other things too of a like nature. Please remember I had no idea DHL was ill. On the morning of the day he died, he suddenly said to me, as distinctly as if he had been here in the room with me: 'Can you remember only the pain and none of the joy?' And his voice was so full of reproach that I made haste to assure him that I *did* remember the joy. Then later on in a strange confused way he said—'What has it all been about?'

The next morning I was busy with my housework when suddenly the room was filled with his presence and for a moment I saw him just as I had known him in early days, with the little cap on the back of his head. That momentary presence was so full of joy that I simply concluded it was an earnest of a real meeting in the near future. I remember saying to myself, 'Now I *know* we're going to meet.'

The following day his death was announced in the paper, and was a terrible shock to me. I give you this for what it is worth...smile it away, if you will, it doesn't matter; the experience was just as real as the fact that I am now holding a pen. I don't think it was self-suggestion, because I didn't know he was ill; I was full of anxiety on his behalf, but I judged his trouble to be of the soul.

I am sure that he broke through his prison before the end, and died a free spirit, though he had lived in bondage. I think his last poems show that he found the way to freedom and wholeness, so that he achieved a triumph, but not the kind that he used to write about so much. It had been my conviction all along that he would find out what the trouble really was, and I had almost dared to believe that having achieved the inner unity, without which he spent himself in vain, he would be strong enough to reshape his life on positive values; but it was not to be. By the time he understood his malady he had spent his vital force. I was expecting too much from one earthly span; the suffering of self-division of the utmost limit was a life-time's work, maybe. The story of the unification lies in the future.

So you see this is how DHL appears to me, and his long arguments about aristocrats and democrats and the rest are only the dusty miles he covered in his pilgrimage. The only interest they have for me is the internal evidence they bear as to the state of his soul. Apart from that they are utterly unreal. There is no such thing as a division of people into aristocrats and democrats; it is the same with human beings as with the wheat among which the enemy had sown tares. 'Let both grow together till harvest.' The only definition of democracy that appeals to me is this: 'Democracy is that arrangement of society in which every individual has an opportunity of becoming an aristocrat.... 'By their fruits ye shall know them.'

Again, is that Golden Age of which DHL dreamed in some remote past any further back than his own boyhood and youth? It is a great error to suppose that his early life was unhappy. In our home his name was a synonym for joy—radiant joy in simply being alive. He communicated that joy to all of us, and made us even happy with one another while he was there; no small achievement in a family like ours! No, DHL's Golden Age was the time up to nineteen or so, before that fatal self-division began to manifest itself. What was it Keats said about a great man's life being an allegory, and his works the comments upon it? Something of that applies to DHL. You see that in essentials my feeling for him has not changed in spite of other deep affection. What he said about the indestructibility of love is quite true, on a particular plane.

NOTES

For a note on Jessie Chambers, see p. 31. A version of this letter was printed in Helen Corke's book on Jessie Chambers (see p. 31), pp. 39–46.

1. Helen Corke's study of Lawrence's *Apocalypse*; see p. 78.

2. 'The End' (originally titled 'Memories'), 'The Bride' ('The Dead Mother' is another version of the same poem), and 'The Virgin Mother', all published in *Amores* (1916).

3. The reference is to a moving letter written by Lawrence on 14 November 1928 to J. D. (David) Chambers, the brother of Jessie. It concludes, 'whatever else I am, I am somewhere still the same Bert who rushed with such joy to the Haggs' (*Letters*, p. 762).

Index